THE GREENING OF BUSINESS

The Greening of Business

edited by

Rhys A. David

Gower

in association with BUSINESS Magazine

Published by
Gower Publishing Company Limited
Gower House
Croft Road
Aldershot
Hants   GU11 3HR
England

Gower Publishing Company
Old Post Road
Brookfield
Vermont   05036
USA

British Library Cataloguing in Publication Data
The Greening of business.
    1. Economic conditions, related to environment
    I. David, Rhys
    330.9

    ISBN 0–566–07281–5

Printed in Great Britain at the University Press, Cambridge

Contents

List of Figures

Notes on the Contributors

Kenneth Collins is MEP for Strathclyde East and Chairman of the European Parliament's Environment Committee.

Jeff Fergus is Managing Director of Leo Burnett Research.

Chris Hampson is an Executive Director of ICI and Chairman of the CBI's Environment Committee.

Gordon McCartney is Secretary of the Association of District Councils.

The Rt Hon. Christopher Patten MP was at the time of the Conference Secretary of State for the Environment.

David Pearce is Professor of Economics at University College London, Director of the London Environmental Economics Centre and special adviser to the Secretary of State for the Environment.

Reginald Watts is Chairman of The Watts Group.

John Wybrew is a Director of Shell (UK) Ltd and served as a member of the Prime Minister's Policy Unit under Mrs Thatcher, whilst on secondment from Shell (UK) Ltd.

Preface

The Greening of Business – the title of the BUSINESS Magazine conference in late 1990, and of this book, based on papers given at that conference by environmentalists, industrialists, politicians, and consumer experts – says it all. The 1990s will see a gathering of pace in a process that began to get under way in the latter half of the last decade, leading, it now seems likely, to significant changes in the way industry carries out its operations.

The realization that the needs of the present generation have to be balanced by efforts to protect the needs and interests of future generations, has been a long time a-building, but now permeates industrial, political, and consumer, as well as academic thinking in all the economically advanced nations, and in many less well-endowed countries as well. Industry has to change its ways, as many of the best companies, large and small, have come to accept. Legislation is being strengthened, and the polluter will increasingly be made to pay. Companies that fail to act now may eventually find they have left it too late, as pressure builds up not just from the UK authorities, but from the European Commission as well.

The publication as far back as 1962 of Rachel Carson's book, *The Silent Spring*, was clearly a seminal development, but the event that perhaps first made environmental problems impinge seriously on the wider public consciousness was the Chernobyl nuclear disaster. The public itself had a nasty shock but others were even more directly affected, and remain so, even as far afield as Britain. There is no need to tell farmers in Wales, Scotland or the English Lake District, the movement of whose sheep is in some cases still under restriction, that environmental problems can now have hemispheric, or even global, dimensions.

Coming on top of this, there has been a welter of scientific reports on global warming as a result of carbon dioxide emissions, and on the apparent danger to the ozone layer from the release of chlorofluorocarbons. Coupled with a perceptible rise in both winter and summer temperatures – whether as a consequence or not is still unknown – these problems have alerted the public to the fragility of the planet we inhabit.

If the politicians in the traditional parties were in any doubt as to whether or not they should react, this same public sent them a very clear signal in the 1989 Euroelection, when 15 per cent of the vote in the UK (and similar proportions elsewhere) went to the Green Party. Though the tide has since ebbed again for the Green Party, this is not least because the other parties have moved swiftly to steal their clothes.

As the White Paper produced by Christopher Patten (the then UK Environment Secretary), in the autumn of 1990 suggests, the Conservative Government appreciates that the environment will be one of the key issues in the first British general election of the 1990s. Indeed, as Mr Patten makes clear in his chapter, the government is now itself largely committed to the philosophy of sustainable development. Labour has been quick, too, to establish its own green credentials with its own more far-reaching agenda, and the third force in British politics, the Liberal Democrats, were, of course, campaigning on green issues long before the other two parties. Though the main parties will differ on the relative weight to be given to regulation or market forces, the need for action is accepted. Domestic parliaments, as another chapter makes clear, are being moved along, too, by European Community legislation.

As two of the chapters in the book demonstrate, industry has become increasingly aware of its responsibilities and of the growing pressures from customers and regulators. Whereas many bigger companies might at one stage have been criticized for token environmentalism – cosmetic policies developed with an eye to the public relations benefit – the best are now much more likely to seek to build an environmental action programme into their operations as a whole. Shell, as John Wybrew points out in his contribution, has set itself the task of achieving 'zero negative impact' for its operations. It is trying to do this through total commitment from board room to shop floor, through a comprehensive environment policy setting out clearly defined objectives, through attempts to engineer good environmental practice into day-to-day business, through environmental auditing, and through a policy of transparency with the public and authorities. For

Shell, as another contributor, Chris Hampson makes clear, read also ICI. And where big companies lead, their smaller brethren are likely to follow.

Local authorities are keen to help, as the spokesman for one of their UK-wide associations reports, and would welcome a more cordial relationship with business to replace the confrontational stand-off which has so often characterized dealings in the past. Industry should, they urge, be willing to take a pro-active approach to environmental matters, taking steps, perhaps in conjunction with the local authority, to prevent problems arising.

In adopting this much more concerned stance, industry and government find themselves in harmony with public opinion, which at many levels of society is now demanding action to safeguard the planet for future generations. For many people, Jeff Fergus points out, 'green' concerns have become an important part of everyday life. At the level of the ordinary consumer, the great success of, for example, the Body Shop, in Britain has demonstrated that there is a market for environmentally friendly non-exploitative products. And spurred on by consumer sentiment, consumer product giants like Unilever and Procter & Gamble have moved quickly to reduce the environmental impact of many of their products and have cut down on unnecessary packaging. Other companies have stepped up research into products and processes which will help industry clean up its act.

Yet, for all the good intentions of industry revealed in these pages, and for all the positive encouragement now coming from the consumer, the action needed in the UK or Europe has by no means yet been secured and remains a hostage to other considerations. The recession, and the threat it has already posed to jobs, provides plausible grounds for bearing less heavily than might otherwise be the case on companies, the environmental standards of which need to be upgraded, as trade associations will no doubt be arguing with increasing vigour during the present economic slowdown. The squeeze on consumer incomes as a result of rising unemployment and high UK interest rates will discourage many consumers from choosing the more expensive, but environmentally less damaging, options when they make their purchases.

Oil prices, over the medium and long term, will stay high as a result of the Gulf War. This will encourage essential conservation, but put further pressure on consumers and industry. The Gulf War brought massive damage to the environment and caused huge losses of oil which can never be replaced. Finally, local authorities and others charged with supervising environmental regulations can only do so if they have the resources, and for these they are in competition with other claimants on the public purse, such as education and health.

These dilemmas and doubts remain, but if one message comes clearly through from the cases put by all the contributors to this book it is that the first stage of the battle – raising consciousness – has been won and that there is now a general acceptance that, as the then Prince of Wales said in the 1930s in another context, 'something must be done'.

The BUSINESS Magazine conference, ably chaired by Joe Rogaly, associate editor and political columnist of the *Financial Times*, has, it is hoped, set out the issues and exposed a commitment to action and a degree of consensus – despite some differences of emphasis – which must surely now be built on. This certainly was the view of many of those who posed questions – information-seeking, point-making and speaker-challenging – from the floor. Their contribution, too, is included in these pages, representing very largely as they do the opinions of those who will ultimately carry the burden within industry of implementing decisions taken at political and boardroom level.

The conference, and this book arising out of it, represent BUSINESS Magazine's own contribution to the debate, and mirror the interest our writers have rightly taken in the topic in the five years since the magazine was launched. Much of what appears in BUSINESS each month centres on companies that have successfully penetrated market sectors or transformed unpromising prospects, and, in many instances, the thread running through such stories has been environmental awareness. As the 1990s progress, this is a theme which is certain to recur increasingly in many of the stories yet to appear.

Rhys David   February 1991
Publisher
BUSINESS Magazine

Acknowledgements

The editor and publishers wish to thank the following for permission to reproduce copyright material.
The Automobile Association, for Figure 5.3, from 1990.
Leo Burnett UK and USA Research, for Figures 5.4–5.10.
World Bank, for Figure 6.5, from *World Population Projections, 1987–8*.

1 Environmentalism and Business

Professor David Pearce

A second 'environmental revolution' is already well under way. The first was in the 1970s, when our knowledge of environmental science was less but the threats to the standard of living and quality of life appeared no less real than they do today. The talk then was of 'limits to growth' – both population and economic growth – and the widely canvassed prescription was to surrender growth in favour of an alternative low-technology lifestyle in symbiosis with nature. What we might call 'lifestyle environmentalism' has not gone away, and the presence of the Green Party and a few of the more extreme environmental groups reminds us of its existence; but it has given substantial ground to a more acceptable form of environmentalism based on the philosophy of **sustainable development**. It is this philosophy which pervades the second environmental revolution.

Although some people feel it is not possible to define 'sustainable development', I do not think it is so problematic. The prefix 'sustainable' is there to urge us to think of forms of economic and social progress that are enduring, long-lasting and which take account of the probable interests of future generations. The term 'development' certainly includes in it the idea of a rising material standard of living and rising real *per capita* incomes. But 'development' is wider in scope, and draws our attention to the need to embrace values which include **self-respect** and **sensitivity to others** – including other species, basic freedoms, educational achievement, and mental and bodily health. Defined this way, sustainable development

1

scarcely looks like something anyone could disapprove of; yet politicians are reluctant to endorse it, often preferring to substitute 'sustainable growth' for 'sustainable development'. There is, then, some little way to go in persuading everyone of the virtues of sustainable development, but the force of international opinion is now unquestionably behind it.

Casual empiricism suggests that the 1970s' environmental revolution expired in world recession, largely induced by OPEC oil price increases. An equally casual look into the future might suggest that history will repeat itself. The high oil prices that have come with the Gulf crisis of 1990–1 and the increasing number of projections of world recession might be taken as precursors to the end of this second revolution. I do not believe this will be the case. The first environmental revolution never died out: it was like a ratchet effect – we moved several rungs up the ladder of environmental consciousness, and the environmentally conscious moved into positions of respectability. I think that this explains in part one of the phenomena of the modern-day environmentalism – the **green employee**. Talking to business in 1989–90 I was impressed by the number of occasions on which I was told that the real pressure to be green was coming not from environmental pressure groups, or even from the green consumer: it was coming from **inside business**. Business is therefore already reacting to this pressure.

My feeling is that the current revolution will take us a few more steps up the green ladder, and that this time it will be the **educational system** that will provide the ratchet. While I might expect my children to be environmentally more conscious than their fellow students, given the pervasive role that environmental discussion has in our household, I am impressed by the fact that much of what they learn does not come from their parents but from their school. I am convinced, therefore, that the new environmentalism will persist, even when the more strident rhetoric has died away.

Economics and the New Environmentalism

Another change has been taking place in environmental policy, although it has so far attracted less attention than the many environmental 'scare stories', real and imagined. In *Blueprint for a Green Economy* (Pearce *et al.*, 1989) my colleagues and I called for radical reappraisal of the way that the UK tries to achieve its environmental goals. We called first and foremost for a change in the way that environmental statistics are presented – not as adjuncts to other statistics, but as an integral part of the **management of the economy**. We did not recommend changing the GNP statistics, although I believe that this will happen in due course, but we stressed the need to show how **environmental** change was firmly linked to **economic** change. In the 1990 White Paper on environment, *This Common Inheritance,* the government announced that it would be presenting comprehensive environmental statistics on a regular basis.

In *Blueprint* we also called for changes in the way in which public policies, investment projects and investment programmes are **evaluated**. In 1990 the government announced guidelines for the modification of these appraisals, guidelines which stressed the importance of the environment. *Blueprint* also called for the introduction of market-based instruments – weapons for environmental control which rely on altering the **structure of incentives in the market place**. Such incentives might be environmental taxes, but there are dozens of potential instruments, ranging from deposit-refund systems through to user charges and tradeable permits. Which instrument is best used in which circumstances requires careful evaluation, and some critics of the White Paper were naive in expecting the announcement of such measures in a White Paper on the environment. What the White Paper did announce was that the government was giving serious attention to the evaluation of such instruments; that is as it should be. Annex A discussed levies on tyres; on the potential for the National Rivers Authority (NRA) and HM Inspectorate of Pollution (HMIP) to introduce discharge- and emission-related charges; land dereliction taxes; aircraft noise taxes; and tradeable permits for acid rain control. The White Paper also entertained the introduction of carbon taxes and/or tradeable permits in order to achieve a CO_2 target of the kind announced by the Prime Minister, Mrs Margaret Thatcher, in 1990. Such taxes on stationary energy sources, we are told, will not be introduced in the next few years; transport, however, is quite explicitly exempted from this undertaking.

Business needs to know that market-based instruments are under consideration. Some, of course, are coming into play – as with rising landfill charges and the introduction of 'recycling credits' whereby recyclers can claim avoided landfill costs from the disposers of waste.

The measures being contemplated in the UK are also being contemplated (and some have already been introduced) in OECD Europe and Scandinavia. In a review of these measures (Pearce, 1989), I found that all countries apart from Spain were looking at environmental taxes, though few appeared to be taking tradeable permits seriously. Even in Greece and Portugal, air pollution taxes were being evaluated, and at the Rome Summit in 1990 the EC member countries requested the Commission in Brussels to draw up guidelines on a number of such taxes, including a carbon tax.

This, then, is the prospect for environmental policy in the 1990s. It will, in my view, blend direct regulation and economic instruments in an effort to secure a more efficient approach to modern-day problems.

What Should Business Do?

In recent months, a new willingness to listen to arguments about the economic approach to environmental policy has become apparent. Two features of this approach are particularly interesting for business.

First, because the economic approach is more efficient, my belief is that a regulatory system that relies on **market-based approaches** will generally be less onerous for industry – both in terms of administrative intervention by government, and financially. It is well established in the economic literature that taxes and tradeable permits keep the costs of complying with regulation to a minimum.

Second, **environmental taxes** have as their purpose the removal of a distortion in the economy; this distortion arises from the fact that the continued presence of unacceptable pollution and waste means that we are not paying enough for the environment. The use of environmental taxes is one of the means whereby this distortion is corrected. If the taxes induce **technological change** towards cleaner production processes, then the tax is avoided, but in the short run at least the taxes will raise revenues for government. These revenues need not stay in the Exchequer: they can be recycled back to industry (and the public) by reducing taxes that act as disincentives to effort: a tax on vehicles or fuel could be used to reduce corporation tax, for example.

If environmental policy is to be driven increasingly by the use of economic incentives, then there is a twofold challenge for industry.

First, it is essential for business to learn the **language of environmental economics**; that cannot be difficult given the well-qualified nature of the many industrial economists in UK industry, although it is often the line manager in charge of safety and environment who will have to learn the new dialogue. Second – and assuming of course that the arguments are as persuasive as I believe them to be – the industrial lobby needs to welcome, and call for, the introduction of the market-based approach. It needs to combine that call with pressure to use the proceeds of environmental taxes to **reduce distortionary taxation elsewhere in the economy**.

This challenge requires industry to learn – and then engineer – a **change in policy**. This is quite different to the challenge that arises if industry enters the 'reactive' mode where governments legislate and industry protests, modifies the regulatory imposition, and sits back to wait for the next round of legislation. Above all, if (as I believe) future environmental policy is characterized by green taxes, recycling incentives, and tradeable permits, industry needs to know **now** how it will respond to the new environmental policy.

Industry can – and should – engage in 'self-regulation'. **Environmental audits** are in vogue, procedures whereby industry assesses itself (or is assessed by others) for its **environmental friendliness**. These are valuable as a self-learning process, but are of limited use if they are not linked to a system of **incentives within industry** to reward environmental achievement: otherwise I fear we face the prospect of ecological whitewash – or a 'greenwash' as it might be called. Environmental audits reveal some surprises – profits can, to some extent, be increased by close inspection of energy and materials usage.

Self-regulation brings a further potential gain, and it could be a very large one. We know that the single biggest policy measure to contain global warming will be energy conservation; we also know that, if the world is serious about global warming, we will not achieve its control by 'good housekeeping' alone. My personal belief is that the **taxation of greenhouse gases**, or something akin to taxation, is inevitable. The White Paper itself noted that the UK CO_2 reduction target would not be achieved without such measures. But self-regulation by industry, combined with the kind of lobbying pressure already mentioned, could minimize the disruptive effects of a carbon tax.

I see, then, an environmental strategy for industry as a whole. It consists of a two-pronged advance in which the plea for efficient environmental policy is combined with a demand for tax reform and the offer of environmental **self-regulation**. But the ultimate challenge for business is the same as the challenge to all of us: stop treating nature as if the little we spend on it should command respect. It has taken over 100 years to stop treating people as if their health and wellbeing were costless; now we acknowledge it as a fact of life, and the costs of maintaining and improving health are borne by individuals and the state. All of us now need to accelerate the same transition for nature.

Questions and Answers

Q   Barry Higgs   (Fertilizer Manufacturers' Association)
    Could you say, as an economist, whether you agree with the general
    principle that many people put forward, that the money raised from
    taxes on particular activities should be devoted specifically to those

activities, or to corresponding aspects of the environment? This is contrary to the view the Treasury always puts forward, that money is not collected for a specific purpose – it goes into the general revenue, as it were. Do you think it is valid for people to pursue this particular line?

A   If you want to pursue it strategically with Her Majesty's Treasury I would recommend giving up now, because you won't get what the economists would call an earmarking argument past the Treasury! Their case would be that it introduces yet further distortions in the economy. If you raise a pound by taxing fertilizers – and I hasten to add that is something I have never recommended – and then it has to be given back somehow to the agricultural sector, the argument is that that may not be, as it were, the most efficient use of that pound; you may be introducing a further economic distortion. This could get quite serious if, for example, you started to raise very large sums of money in carbon taxes and then had to argue that the whole revenue, which could run into billions, should be given back to – the electricity industry or to transport. So 'earmarking' as such will tend not to get very much support from government economists, and they have a fairly sound theoretical case. 'Earmarking' of the kind I mentioned is slightly different. It's not so much 'earmarking' as 'revenue neutrality' – that is to say, you raise money by means of a tax and return it by lower taxes on other distortionary elements in the economy. All of that said, if you look at the actual environmental taxes in place – and user charges in the OECD countries – until very recently earmarked taxes dominated. They were taxes where (say) the pulp and paper industry would be faced with some charge, which would then be collected and recycled back into pollution abatement equipment. There are some economic arguments for doing that, but they are not terribly powerful in terms of cost-effective effort. I would argue against lobbying for this at the moment.

Q   Samuel Radcliffe (British Cast Metals' Industry Research Association) Having come from a fairly green Greater London Council, I am very impressed with the consciousness and awareness of the industrialists I have met. They do have a problem however: in a business which is highly cost competitive, increased environmental controls will tend to drive foundry activities to southern European countries (such as Portugal), where the environmental requirements are much less stringent than in the UK. This could give an advantage to other developing countries (Eastern countries, such as Turkey, which is already planning for an increase in our type of business). Now this is obviously going to affect the manufacturing base in the UK. Has Professor Pearce a solution to this problem?

A   There are no easy solutions to that one; it's a familiar problem. As everybody knows, of the two examples you have given Portugal is already in the EC, and Turkey has every chance of becoming a member. It would be strategically unwise to relocate in either country if you look at the nature of environmental legislation, and in 1992 we shall have to start talking about harmonization of environmental standards in order to stop exactly that kind of process taking place. If, on the other hand, we were to substitute somewhere like Thailand for Portugal or Thailand for Turkey the case might well be a more powerful one. Bear in mind, however, that environmental regulations do not represent a large part of costs, so it would be odd for industry to move in response to environmental regulation alone. I don't doubt for a moment that this is true for some industries where environmental regulations can cause very significant increases in cost – we have, for example, seen the cement industry in the United States moving out, but there is a bottom line to all of that. The trade-off is quite explicit: if we want a cleaner environment, and that deters certain industries from setting up here, then that makes it very clear what the price of that environment is – it is the foregone income or foregone employment that arises from keeping dirty industry in existence. No one would suggest that you get environmental benefits for nothing; they cost money. The real political issue is whether or not we are already willing to pay for that environmental benefit. So it may well be that you have to let certain polluting industries go from the areas where you keep environmental qualities very high in favour of countries where there is a lower willingness to pay for environmental quality. However, much of my work is in the developing world, and I see the emergence of quite strict environmental standards in a number of countries. So it would be quite difficult to judge where there were going to be permanently lower standards compared to the standards of the EC. If it were my money, I would probably stay where I was!

Q   Nicholas von Baillou (United Research Ltd)
    Your market-based approach, looking at potential taxation as an economic vehicle as opposed to a punitive device is fascinating. Have you had the opportunity of doing research into improving the actual

manufacturing processes option? There is, for instance, some evidence in the USA that companies took legislation seriously because it could be quite punitive; they have addressed this by significantly improving profitability without buying a lot of expensive capital equipment, and similarly have been able to reduce their effluence and discharges into the air by such substantial percentages as to demonstrate that this approach is more efficacious than some had assumed.

A   I think that this is one of the most powerful arguments for the market-based instrument. If we look at the way regulations operate, you can always set an environmental standard in such a way that you force the polluter to introduce better and better technology. You can do that by setting your technological requirement just a little bit above what is actually available, or easy to get at. That way, you can have a technological incentive. But it isn't a terribly powerful one, whereas one of the virtues of the market-based approach is that it offers what I call a 'continuous irritant' to the polluter: the tax is always going to be there but you can avoid it, and you can avoid it by first of all looking at in-place equipment and seeing what you can do to reduce the ratio of emissions to industrial output: it forces you into that way of thinking. It may also force you into looking very actively for more advanced technology which reduces levels of emission. You asked whether research had been done. I don't know of any in the UK that would substantiate my belief, but I know that experience in the USA bears out what you say: I see that as one further virtue of the market-based system.

Q   Timothy Hornsby (Nature Conservancy Council)
In a feature on fish farming, in the October 1990 issue of *Business Magazine*, it was stated that the White Paper had suggested that the marine consultation areas introduced in Scotland should also be extended to England and Wales. If one is looking at a balance between regulations and market incentive will there not be a continuing requirement for some sort of planning strategy, some sort of indicative planning, as with marine fish farming?

A   Nothing I have said should be taken as implying that you can engage in environmental policies using solely marked-based instruments. That never was the argument in *Blueprint for a Green Economy* — nor, of course, is that the view taken in the White Paper. There will always be a role for land uses, protected areas and so on; that is part of the regulatory process. At the moment, virtually all environmental policies are implemented through those kinds of procedures – land use planning, for example. I push for the market-based instruments' approach because it doesn't get a significant look in at the moment other than through things like the difference in leaded and unleaded petrol prices and the forthcoming changes in waste management policy. So in terms of my interest in getting a point of view across, I am going to carry on pushing for the market-based approach, and I have not seen anything to lead to me to change my view. In future, as in the past there will always be a role for what I would call 'direct regulations', including land use planning procedures.

Q John Garbutt (Nicholson, Graham and Jones)
The paper published in July 1990 by the Institute of Fiscal Studies (IFS) on the impact of green taxes seemed to suggest that such taxes will fall hardest on the poor. Have you any comment on this?

A If you hypothesize on environmental tax, and then simply look at the incidence of it – particularly the incidence of a tax on energy – then of course you discover that the poorer will pay a bigger percentage of their income out in the form of environmental taxation than will the richer person. There are several problems with this. One is that the IFS did not actually look at the detailed ways in which you could offset that burden on lower income groups; we have a large number of mechanisms that we could use within the social security system and within the taxation system, so it shouldn't be too difficult to devise a system of taxation which is not regressive in that sense. The other point is more subtle, and is also not addressed in the IFS study. We are not talking about environmental policy versus doing nothing – at least I hope we're not. No one is arguing that there should not be controls on CO_2 emissions; the argument is about how you do it. Suppose we introduced a regulation tomorrow saying 'thou shalt not emit more than such-and-such a level of carbon dioxide': that imposes a cost on industry, just as any other regulation imposes a cost on industry. So in part – not 100 per cent, but in part – industry bears some of the cost and the consumer bears some of the cost as well. Any regulation has an impact on prices, which has an impact on the consumer; so any regulation can be regressive. The difference is that the environmental tax, in terms of potential regressiveness, is explicit: you can see it. But what gets hidden in the regulatory process, particularly from the consumer, is the idea that somehow regulations have no cost. They do have a cost, they are passed on, it is simply that it is not as obvious as it is in the case of an environmental tax. So on those two grounds I'd say yes, we know some taxes are going to be regressive; I believe the tax system can be designed in such a way as to offset that regressiveness, and in any event all regulation is going to have a regressive element if we are not careful about how we design it. It is much more difficult to offset the regressiveness of a regulation as opposed to a market-based instrument.

References

Chemicals in a Green World (1990) (London, Chemical Industries' Association).

Pearce, D. (1989) **New Environmental Policies**, Recent OECD Country Experience and its Relevance to the Developing World (Paris, OECD Development Centre, forthcoming).

Pearce, D., *et al.* (1989) *Blueprint for a Green Economy* (London: Earth Scan).

This Common Inheritance (1990) Cmd 1200 (London, HMSO).

The Distributional Consequences of Environmental Taxes (1990) (London, IFS).

2 What Government Expects From Business

Rt Hon. Christopher Patten MP

The 1990 Environment White Paper has set out the principles by which we believe Britain can best approach the environmental challenges ahead. How are we now to proceed, and what do we expect of business in this process? I want to explore some of the principles from the White Paper which will provide the key to future work on the environment, and then consider how business can play its part in turning these into practice.

There are both challenges and opportunities ahead for business: 'green' consumerism (see Chapter 5), new markets abroad (especially in Eastern Europe), and demands for technical change provide the **opportunities**. Every firm will need to have a full understanding of those potential markets. Increasing environmental awareness and the need for tighter controls over pollution provide the **challenges** to every industry. Each industry must understand the implications for its own processes of the new environmental agenda; there is a range of issues presenting a range of different problems and opportunities for different industries. If we lose sight of that, we are in danger of adopting policies which give a patina of 'environmentalism' but do not go to the heart of our organizations.

General Principles

I want to begin with the five general principles of the government's environmental policy: stewardship; sound science; precaution; access to information; and action for all. They are good principles. If there is a general expectation of business, it is that they should aim to embrace these same principles.

Stewardship

Stewardship is the cornerstone of the government's approach. It commits the government to bequeathing to future generations a **healthy and viable environment**. This is the principle of 'sustainable development' – ensuring that our rush for change or profit, or simply our carelessness, does not diminish our natural resources. It is a duty we all owe future generations. This is an ethical question for us all – for business no less than for government and individuals. But I know that business wishes to play its part in improving the environment, for the same reasons that we all as individuals cherish our environmental heritage.

Sound Science

'Sound Science' means making sure we get our **environmental decisions right**. Environmental questions are not simple, and answers are rarely costless; we should go not for token gestures but for steps which actually contribute. Failure to do this will lead to troubles in the future, while creating costs for the present.

The burdens this government will impose on business will be fair ones, reflecting the costs on both sides of the equation in ending environmental damage. I am confident that the various industries will continue the current cooperation in determining what is the best scientific approach to problems. Honest and full cooperation is the best way to place Britain in a strong position with its competitors: the example of West Germany is often quoted, where industry has benefited from working towards regulation. The government will not allow costs to industry to dissuade it from the need to protect the environment but we must make sure that the decisions we take are the most cost-effective ones.

Precaution

'Precaution' involves making sure we take measures at the **right time**. Putting off decision-taking only stores up problems for the future, which will mean greater costs ahead; we must act before problems become too severe. This makes the best sense for business, too: too often UK industry is seen as **reactive**, or opposing necessary change. The government intends to take increasingly positive and advanced positions in European and international dealings; industry will need to play its part in allowing us to take the lead abroad – but the benefits will be substantial if we can take these opportunities.

Access to Information

Such access is one of the themes of the White Paper which I hope will deliver the most. Lack of information breeds **fear** and **misunderstanding**; open information brings **pressure where it is due**. The government will be publishing regular statistical reports which will allow people to hold it to account for any failings in pursuing the goals it has set itself. Increased access to information on discharges, as proposed in the Environmental Protection Bill,[1] can do much the same for business.

I firmly believe all this will be an aid to dialogue and to better understanding. At the same time we will be pursuing environmental and energy **labelling schemes** – hopefully on a Europe-wide basis; these will confirm the public's increasing willingness to act to improve the environment in their daily decisions.

Action for All

If we are to make sustainable development fundamental to the way we live, then we all need to play our full part in **delivering environmental improvement**; the final Chapter of the White Paper lists action for individuals, local government and businesses. We will all need to weigh the environment in all our activities; for business, that means having corporate environmental strategies, policies and practices. The government has itself set up coordinating mechanisms and is preparing new guidance to work towards a corporate approach to the environment in its own affairs; such a corporate approach to the environment is simply part of **good management**. This guidance is in addition to the Department of Trade and Industry's (DTI) existing business and environment advice. The Department of the Environment and the DTI will also be increasing their efforts on a regional basis to develop business interest in the environment, which will complement the excellent work the CBI is doing to take the environmental message beyond the capital.

Developing Policies

Close and positive contact with business is essential for getting the right balance in our future action on the environment; the White Paper already includes many proposals for specific action. There are still more areas where government wishes to explore the best way ahead. Business has already played a full part in developing such areas as the Best Available Techniques Not Entailing Excessive Costs (BATNEEC) approach to pollution control in the Environmental Protection Bill; we now want similar close involvement in deciding the best way ahead in other areas. There are a number of key areas to develop if we want to move further towards the goal of sustainable development; we need to ensure that our approach is right.

Involving Business

The White Paper set out a whole series of environmental priorities; these represent a considerable programme. The government wishes to ensure that in developing these major themes over the coming years, and in implementing its programme for environmental improvement, business is fully involved at all stages. There is already a long tradition of close cooperation with industry in the development of **standards**; this must continue if we are to ensure that the best methods are adopted, and this will demand a positive contribution from the different industries concerned.

We will continue to consult business on topics of interest at the earliest possible stage, especially in developing issues on the international front; but we need a more interactive and creative approach. This is why a new body is being created to advise on strategic environmental issues as they affect business. To help the dialogue with business further the Department of Trade and Industry will shortly be producing a guide to who does what in government; this will offer business a clear list of **contacts on environmental issues**, and be of particular use to smaller businesses who wish to keep abreast of environmental developments.

Choosing the Right Methods

A subject of increasing importance is the balance between the use of **market-based** instruments and of **regulation**. Regulation has long been the traditional approach to controlling environmental impacts, but we all know that regulation has its drawbacks; it can lack flexibility and, if it is not very carefully devised, can create distortions in the market which can even harm the environment it is meant to protect. The White Paper demonstrates clearly that government believes in a balanced use of regulation and of the market. Regulation has a place – indeed the Environmental Protection Bill[1] has introduced some of the strongest environmental protection legislation in Europe. But that regulation needs to work **with the grain of**

the market, and with **the help of the market**. If we get the price signals right in the market, we have the most efficient method of shaping our environment.

Let me take the Environmental Protection Bill as an example of the way that regulation, flexibly used together with market mechanisms, can best serve our environmental needs. First, BATNEEC gives us a flexible approach to **pollution control**. This is an area where the standards will naturally evolve with technological developments. Integrated pollution control (IPC) provides us with a system which prevents one of the worst aspects of regulation — that in order to meet some regimes other elements are allowed to suffer. IPC means lowering the environmental impact to a minimum across all the different areas of possible pollution. The system also has its market elements. HM Inspectorate of Pollution (HMIP) will charge to recover the costs of giving licences under the new system, and in time we hope to extend the charging regime here (and for the National Rivers Authority) to include **incentive charging** — higher costs to discourage excess pollution.

The Environmental Protection Bill also allows for absolute standards to be applied: I will be able to direct that permissions granted enable us to meet overall standards (for example, EC standards) for environmental quality. Of course the Bill is only part of this process. Elsewhere we will be looking for an even stronger market role. This is particularly important when we come to some of the major issues facing the planet, such as the use of carbon fuels; if we are to tackle the problem of global warming, then in the long term it is likely that the relative prices of fuel and energy will have to rise.

There was some disappointment, in environmental circles at least, that the White Paper did not include the introduction of some form of 'carbon tax'. For the longer term, this cannot be off our agenda entirely; but the steps we take to address global problems must be part of concerted international action. This government will not shirk from imposing necessary costs, but we will not use the market in the UK to place our own business at a grave competitive disadvantage.

There is much work still to be done in this field — on the potential for tradeable permits, for example, or on the way in which we price the environment more generally in our investment and infrastructure decisions. But there is no question that we should seize the dynamic opportunities offered by market-based instruments to build a strong but flexible approach to working towards sustainable development. I very much hope that industries will continue to play a positive role in developing ideas for the use of the market in environmental protection.

New Markets

I have mentioned the challenges posed by global warming and the need for an international approach. Here, if anywhere, is an opportunity for business to seize new markets; if we are to help developing countries avoid making the mistakes in profligate use of resources that we ourselves have made in the past, we need to provide technology which will enable them to clean their environment and make most efficient use of those resources. Eastern Europe itself presents us with opportunities for developing our pollution technology in new markets; but the real challenge will be in meeting the needs of less developed countries, who could easily go for the growth they need by exploiting their resource richness. In a whole series of areas – pollution control, forest management, refrigeration, infrastructure provision, and power supply – we need to work to ensure that their growth happens in a way which helps preserve their, and the world's, natural heritage. I would ask industry to seize these opportunities and challenges: they are (as Chapter 7 points out) good for the environment and good for business.

Expectations of Business

What are the government's expectations of business? We hope for a positive input to the continuing debate about the environment we want to have in the UK; we want to see business working to place a greater emphasis on the need for sustainable practices in its own activities: this means greater awareness **corporately** – by staff at all levels – of specific environmental impacts and opportunities of relevance to the organization. We need **openness and public involvement**; we need a commitment to helping achieve our environmental goals – with industry working to a new ethic and showing responsibility in the global challenges ahead.

The Government's Promise

What should you expect of government? With your help, and the help of the environmental movement, we can promise to act to end real problems, with measures targeted on specific needs. We are committed to a continued effective balance between necessary regulation – made as responsive to developing needs and problems as possible – and the market instruments which can help shape more sustainable growth. We can also promise that we will continue to encourage the consumer awareness which has so helped to shape the current debate.

Conclusion

My message is, therefore, threefold:

- **Seize the opportunities** ahead in green technology and green markets.
- **Look ahead in your planning processes** to future developments — environmental change, water pollution, air pollution — and use this planning **creatively**, not just in modernizing plant but even in repositioning the company in its markets.
- Act **positively** to move ahead of these concerns.

Today's environmental issues and problems will not go away. It will be those who tackle them first who will be the market leaders. The White Paper has clearly shown the government's commitment to the environmental path ahead: the road will at times be a steep one, but we must now all move forward along it.

Questions and Answers

Q   Hilary Thompson (National Westminster Bank)
    What role do you see the financial services industry playing in encouraging the 'greening' of industry?

A   Financial services could best help the 'greening' of industry, and the 'greening' of Britain, by playing their part in securing the rapid abatement of inflation, which seems to me to be a necessary and sufficient precondition for sustained economic growth, which in turn seems to me to be a necessary though *not* sufficient condition for a greener environment. Having given you, as it were the 'macro' answer, I would make two proposals, and in doing so recognize that I am speaking to, as it were, my bank manager. First of all I hope that financial services themselves will play a part in helping to develop environmental audit, both for their own activities and for others: it does seem to me that we are all of us (not only government) fairly low on the learning curve in developing environmental audit, and I think that for financial services there is an important role, and one out of which they could make quite a decent profit — we have, for instance, the potential for using the expertise that we can (or should be able to) create for public institutions in this country as part of our aid programme in other countries. I believe myself that one of the most important aspects of technology transfer — which is a much misused phrase since what one is normally talking about are things which are tradeable — is transferring *expertise:* it is difficult to talk about sustaining forestry management unless you have institutions that are capable of managing their environment. Secondly, I hope that financial services will play a part in increasing public knowledge of investment opportunities in firms that are involved with greener technologies. There are many opportunities for tapping 'alleged' consumer interest in greener issues; I think it could usefully be tapped, and could attract some of the investment which a number of new technologies will require. There is an enormous market out there of which we may have, perhaps, 3 per cent. It is obviously growing if you are in German or Japanese industry, and I would like to see Britain doing much better.

Q   Barry Hyman (Marks & Spencer plc)
Marks & Spencer has won an environmental award for its waste recycling initiative, which we intend to go national with — it's environmentally correct, and it will save us money. Do you think we retailers are doing the right things, and doing enough of them, or do you perceive a medium- or long-term need for legislation to make us do more? The Labour Party's environmental initiative includes proposals for control of the national grid, no more nuclear power stations, closure of certain factories and green mortgages to encourage home owners in energy saving. Is there any room here for some sort of consensus across both parties?

A   On legislation to encourage the retail sector to respond even more energetically, both to consumer pressures and the need for financial prudence, I should have thought that the market is going to carry things forward itself. Where we will need I think to intervene (though I hope we can do so in a voluntary way), is with an environmental labelling scheme which attempts to ensure in a 'cradle-to-grave' way that the claims made by manufacturers or retailers for the environmental credentials of products are authentic. I hope myself that those environmental credentials can include packaging; retailers have made many changes in packaging over the last year or two, but I still think we've got further to go: I know that not everything is wrapped like the average shirt, but perhaps far too much is still wrapped like the average shirt rather unnecessarily! I am aware of the boundaries you, and other firms with admirable and improving records like Tesco and Sainsbury, are pushing back. When we produce our action leaflet,[2] indicating how everybody can play a small part in cleaning up the environment, I hope that retailing outlets will agree to stock it at the checkout. I would also like to think that we can agree on an environmental agenda for the UK. It is probably only in the UK that you actually have a serious argument about balancing regulation and market forces as the best way of securing environmental goals. To give one example, we do now have in place an investment programme in cleaning up water which will run at about £2.8 billion a year, found by using the price mechanism. I simply don't believe that it makes sense in these circumstances to spend equally large sums renationalizing the water industry and then to put water investment back into the melting pot as part of the bilateral discussions between a departmental minister and Chief Secretary to the Treasury every year: we know what actually happened to investment in water when we did operate like that. The biggest issues that we have to face relate to the price of energy and the use of energy; they relate immediately to CO_2, and we do have to get beyond short-term populism in dealing with those issues. I simply do not know how you stabilize CO_2 emissions by the year 2000: if you are against nuclear power, if you want to use more British coal, if you are in favour of cutting petrol prices for our cars, that doesn't seem to me to be necessarily a wildly convincing strategy for delivering CO_2 stabilization. It seems to me that there is an agenda which any government of whatever political colour is going to have to face, an agenda which will involve such a government in due course doing things which aren't very popular, like making people pay more for some of the things they have previously taken for granted.

Q   Samuel Radcliffe (British Cast Metals' Industry Research Association) It seems to me that your officials need to be more aware than they appear to be at the moment about the economic impact of what they are proposing at the level of guidance notes. There is the problem in the metal industry of preventing the flight of the industry to shores where environmental conditions are somewhat easier; it seems to me that we could start by being aware of the economic aspects of what we are proposing, and to be more insistent that our colleagues, especially in Europe, perform as well as we do.

A   Let me respond to that in two ways. Much of the environmental debate at a serious level is going to be about whether we are expecting too much of industry, and whether the system of integrated pollution control is putting too many demands on both industry and on the public sector — both in terms of cost and of technological sophistication. One of the unsung (though not inexpensive) heroes in the White Paper is integrated pollution control (IPC). You are also right to say that if it's only the UK that introduces controls as tight over industrial pollution, over emissions to air and water and land, then we put our own industries at a competitive disadvantage. In future Brussels meetings, while not thinking that during the course of a two-hour informal environment council meeting we can harmonize all taxes on energy and introduce a new carbon tax, I shall at least hope that I can press my European colleagues to introduce integrated pollution control themselves; we will be pressing for the sort of IPC introduced in the UK to be introduced right across the Community, and I hope that we will be able to play as central a role in developing it as we are playing, for example, in pressing for an environmental labelling scheme, and as we've already played in developing the Community's hazardous waste policy.

Q   Barry Higgs (Fertilizer Manufacturers' Association)
Voluntary measures, such as codes of best practice and the like, have a very important role to play. For the fertilizer industry, their promotion is almost the only way we can meet our responsibilities for the use of our product. We try to do that as much as we can with regard to farmers and how they use fertilizers; and yet many people believe that that approach is fatally flawed and seem to believe that people will react only for fear of retribution, as it were. What balance do you see in this?

A   One reason why we are faced with, for example, considerable costs in implementing our objectives for water through the National Rivers Authority (NRA) is that one or two good practices were perhaps neglected in the past. Another factor that we have to deal with is the considerable criticism advanced from environmental pressure groups towards anything which looks like good faith and goodwill rather than *binding* regulation. This raises a broader issue: how you can make sensible environmental policy at the moment when so many short-term populist pressures come from the environmental movement – many of them understandable, but not all of them sensible. That is a strong and a powerful argument for improving access to information because it does seem to me that the more information people have in a parliamentary democracy the more likely it is that they will act sanely rather than the reverse, so I do believe very strongly in trying to increase the amount of information in the public sphere. I hope that this will enable us to improve our policy-making process and that that will enable us from time to time to carry conviction when we argue with other people that the best approach is a voluntary one rather than nailing everything down with regulations or laws.

Q   Gareth Jones (Wessex Water Service)
    What role do you think self-regulation will have in improving the green environment?

A   Self-regulation is something which all individuals will have to engage in, from Secretaries of State to Secretaries of State's children taking the bottles to the bottle bank on Sunday mornings! Self-regulation is fine against a background of enforceable codes, but it's not conceivable that in the water environment, for example, we could possibly now say that we are going to achieve all our environmental goals through self-regulation, because there are too many problems associated with the past when the self-regulator was also the regulator. So self-regulation has a part to play, but I think within a framework of clearly articulated regulation onto which a good deal of light is shone. I must add one point. During the passage of the Environmental Protection Bill there was much debate about access to commercial information, and I think I was able to satisfy the House of Commons that even while we thought it was important to keep some things from time to time commercially confidential that didn't mean that we were involved in a big cover-up. We had to dispel doubts and criticisms – I think we were able to do so – but one has to recognize that for the time being those doubts and criticisms exist precisely because we waited rather longer than we should have done – not just in the UK but in all countries – before taking the environment as seriously as it deserves, and as we are now required to take it.

Notes

1. Which received the Royal Assent on 1 November 1990; most of the Environmental Protection Act's provisions came into force on 1 January 1991.

References

This Common Inheritance (1990) Cmd 1200 (London, HMSO).
Wake up! (1991) Department of Environment (London).

3 The EC Perspective

Kenneth Collins MEP

There can be no question at all that environment now is a key area of policy, both in the UK and globally. There is now not a single leader of any country in what we still think of as the free world who has not made a speech about environment policy over the last two or three years. Some surprising people have made speeches about environment policy, some surprising people who even appear to support the idea of having an environment policy, but nonetheless I am all in favour of converts and so I have welcomed the trend. The fact that this conference is being held is remarkable in itself: had you tried to hold such a conference (say) ten years ago, I doubt very much if it would have been all that successful. The mood has changed; opinion polls in the UK and beyond demonstrate the significance of environment policy and both the Conservatives and the Labour Party can see very clearly from their private polls that the general public now puts care of the environment much higher up the agenda than they used to – even in the top two or three issues.

As somebody who has been involved in environmental politics for something like twenty-five years, I find it a very strange experience to be, as it were, in the 'fashionable' bit of my political party. Not only am I in the 'fashionable' bit so far as environment policy is concerned but, after a long time in the wilderness, the party is also suddenly now pro-Europe. The first thing I want to point out is that the EC, like it or not, will have to be the focus for a great deal of environmental thinking in the future. The key areas that I want to consider are first of all the way in which the **scale and locus of environmental decision-making** has changed over the years. Secondly I want to talk about the **democratization** of the EC – and therefore of its environment policy. Thirdly I want to say something about the setting of **political priorities** for environment policy, and how that might be done in the EC.

Scale and Locus of Decision-making

Let me first, then, turn to the scale and locus of environmental decision-making. If you had examined environment policy in the nineteenth century, you would have found that where there was any concern for the environment at all it was very strictly **local**: if smoke went up the chimney its pollution fell on the people immediately around the chimney, and if the water courses became polluted then the people who suffered from cholera and dysentery and so on were in the areas where the water courses were polluted. It was a fairly clear relationship, and the first essays in environment policy, in the UK at any rate, were really the 1875 Public Health Act and various housing interventions in the second half of the nineteenth and even into the beginning of the twentieth century. But by the 1950s, people were beginning to understand that the world was a much more 'inter-related' place than had hitherto been thought. This was an idea which was common enough in University departments of geography, but it wasn't something that I think caught the public imagination. Probably the first time such issues penetrated the public consciousness was when Rachel Carson's book *Silent Spring* was published.[1] Carson's book indicated the general widespread effect of the use of chemicals in agriculture – and how exactly the food chain was affected and how, the food chain having been affected, everything else became affected as well. The activities of what was called the Club of Rome then further popularized the idea that the environment was worth caring about. Their book *Limits to Growth* was published towards the end of the 1960s and basically said that population, energy use and food population were all related at a global level, and they produced predictions which suggested a pretty cataclysmic view of the future. This captured the public imagination, to the point that in 1970 the UK appointed its first standing Royal Commission on environmental pollution, an organization which is still in place and still publishing a good many valuable commentaries on the environmental situation, particularly in the UK. The United Nations convened a conference in Stockholm in 1972, and they again were full of the idea that environment could no longer be treated adequately if it were dealt with at local level – it had now to be dealt with not just at regional level or even national level, it was now a matter of international concern. That recognition has significant **political** implications, because if medium-sized and sometimes even large nation states can no longer tackle environmental problems alone, the **scale of the political unit** required to deal with the environment has to alter as well. And that's where the EC comes in, because although in dealing with environmental policy bilateral agreements might well be possible – that is to say, the UK could sign a series of treaties with France and with Germany and with Spain, or whatever – it becomes a very lengthy process indeed, and you run the risk of the treaty between Britain and France being different from the treaty between Britain and Germany or between Germany and France, and so you get a series of conflicting arrangements rather than the harmony which you might potentially get from EC-wide arrangements.

'Democratization' of the EC

The EC does not assume that each participating party is a gentleman, and the agreements that it reaches do have legislative teeth. The Community is therefore the natural focus of much environmental policy-making – the idea that the nation states can proceed alone is total (and sometimes quite elaborate) fiction. But not all environmental decision-making has to take place at international level, or even at the EC level. One of the buzz words in the Community is **'subsidiarity'**: there are some very big decisions which are appropriately made at a European level; there are others which are perhaps even made at a global level. But there are yet others where the local authority is quite rightly the appropriate level for decision-making so that we have on the one hand the Montreal protocol on CFCs, the intergovernmental panel on climatic change, and international action on global warming, and on the other you have the local authority making quite valid decisions about how the local refuse is to be collected and a number of other things beside: the notion of some kind of European 'superstate' is not on the agenda, even though some people have suggested that it might be. The idea of the European Environment Agency is a perfect example: it will provide a monitoring service for the environment right across Europe, but in order to do that effectively it has to have proper data and it has to be able to say that the data from one country are equivalent to and comparable with data from another. Frankly, the only way that can be done is if the Agency has something of an inspection function, auditing the environmental monitoring methods in each country in a **supervisory** role. The feeling, however, still persists that national governments can tackle the problems alone: 'We can beat these problems. We can change the world and save the world', one UK environmental spokesman said to me. Another said: 'If government, through its own decision-making and institutional structures does not show it means business on the environment, no one else will take the environment seriously'. In eleven years, I have seen twenty-one presidents in office of the Council of Environment Ministers come and go: most come in like lions and go out like Tiggers. I'm not suggesting that the EC is the perfect focus for environmental activity, because frankly it isn't. The first important change in the way the Community tackled the environment policy was in 1979. An environment policy has existed since 20 October 1972 when at the Paris summit of that year the heads of government agreed that such a policy should be drawn up. 1979 saw the first direct elections to the European Parliament – before then the Commission had presented proposals to the delegate Parliament, who commented but argued little. After 1979, there were directly elected MEPs who wanted to be able to go back to their electorate and say: 'This is what I've done'. In 1980 the Italian radical MEP Altiero Spinelli formed a dining club in a restaurant in Strasbourg, the Krokodil Club. They looked at the fact that there was a 'democratic deficit' in the EC – that the Commissioners were accountable to nobody and the ministers were responsible to their own Parliament. The Parliament, on the other hand, which was elected, had no power and so this had to be changed if the Community was going to be a democratic force in the Western world. Spinelli's Krokodil Club led to the Parliament setting up an ad hoc committee on **institutional change**, which eventually produced a document called 'The Draft Treaty of European Union'. In 1983, the Gooch Committee was appointed to consider the whole question of institutional reform: from their deliberations emerged the Single European Act which we all agreed in the Community, and which came into force in 1987. Not bad for a little dining club that apparently had no power and no influence!

Political Priorities for Environment Policy

Even in 1984, I was able to go to my constituency and say 'Yes, it's true the European Parliament has no teeth but over the last five years we've learnt to do quite a lot of damage with our gums'. It was the environment committee of the European Parliament that produced the ban on the import of baby seal skins; the minister said it couldn't be done, but it was done, and they eventually agreed it. The lead-free petrol saga is an interesting one because I remember the then British minister bringing all his civil servants in to talk to three or four of us (an all-party group who went to see him about the possibility of lead-free petrol) and telling us that it wasn't desirable and wasn't necessary. Three months later, after the Royal Commission had reported – and admittedly with a general election in the offing – the same minister called in the same civil servants to tell us that lead-free petrol was highly desirable, absolutely necessary and indeed quite crucial, and please could we support it. And we had to point out that it was our idea in the first place.

Then the 1979 European court case, the *Cassis de Dijon* case held that that which is freely for sale in one country must be freely available for sale in all other countries; that in turn led to the publication of Lord Cockfield's White Paper (1985) on the completion of the internal market, and that, together with the single European Act, changed completely the kind of community that we actually inhabited. The Single European Act introduced environment policy explicitly into the Treaty: up until then, the word 'environment' didn't occur, and you had to cover environment policy via competition policy because the Treaty had been drafted at a time when the environment wasn't a priority. But if you cover environment via competition then you are quite likely to end up with quite severe distortions of your environment. Now we had environment policy built into the Treaty but we also had institutional change because the Single European Act improved the position of the European Parliament, gave us the second reading and insisted on majority voting in the Council of Ministers on certain matters – although not as it happens on environment policy.

If you try to examine how priorities on environment are decided in the Community, you have to look at the interplay of the Commission, the Parliament, and the Council. You could, for example, have an environment policy which was developed at the whim of a commissioner, or perhaps one of his officials; that's a distinct possibility and it is one that I think that some commissioners would like to see. Then, of course, you could have environment policy being developed because of lobbying by very powerful interests; there is no better example of that than the Common Agricultural Policy, and I don't have to explain to you how disastrous that kind of method of arriving at policy is. Then, of course, you could have environment policy arrived at because of the priorities determined by Council presidency. The Council presidency changes every six months and the new president always comes in with his shiny new broom and a new set of priorities, usually paying scant regard to what the priorities of the previous president were, or indeed what they might be of the next one, which quite often makes something of a mess of the work programme which has been agreed painstakingly between the Commision and the Parliament. The worst possible option is to have environment policy developed by civil servants – committees of experts made up of national civil servants sitting in Brussels and making decisions, and later communicating them to the outside world. If you find that fanciful, consider that the Commission proposal for ecological labelling proposes a regulatory committee of national civil servants who by one Article have the power to change the regulations. Once it is appointed, the Commission is accountable basically to itself – what we often have in the Community is a ship with twelve different helmsmen, each with different charts and each apparently seeking a different destination: not clever if you are trying to achieve coherent decision-making. We could try to bring the Community under the control of its people in a way which ensured not only the welfare of its existing population, but also the future of its inhabitants: the North American Indians used to say that we have the planet on loan from our children, and it seems to both my committee and myself that the sooner we place the Community firmly in charge of its elected members, the better. But of course that isn't easy, because trying to get ministers to focus on institutional change is very difficult: they know what's wrong, but trying to get them to deal with it is another matter. One is again drawn to an analogy from A. A. Milne, the opening sentence of *Winnie the Pooh*: '. . . Edward Bear [is] coming downstairs now, bump, bump, bump on the back of his head behind Christopher Robin. It is as far as he knows the only way of coming downstairs but sometimes he feels that there really is another way, if only he could stop bumping for a moment and think of it'.

That is why we have to change the Community, and change it radically. I want to make two suggestions. First of all I think that Article 2 of the Rome Treaty must be amended; the European Community should no longer be committed to growth for its own sake. Growth is desirable – I am not against economic growth; but it must not be bought at the expense of tomorrow's generation. The World Conservation Strategy in 1980 agreed with the idea of sustainable development; Brandt and Bruntland put the idea of sustainable development firmly on the world agenda; the G7 meeting in 1988 included a commitment to sustainable development. When the inter-governmental conference, which began in December 1990, looks at further change in the EC's development, the concept of sustainable development will, I hope, be incorporated in the Treaty.[4] I trust the UK government appreciates how important it is to have this in the Treaty to give us legal commitment in dealing with agricultural policy, energy policy, transport policy, and so on: we cannot have an environment policy in a little watertight compartment; an environment policy has to deal with all the other sectors as well. We need to change not just the economic foundation of the Community, but also its **democratic foundation**, giving the European Parliament a cooperation procedure which allows us to have a second reading, and so on, and to have it introduced for those Articles that deal with environment policy: it is ridiculous that in an area that touches every citizen in the Community the Parliament should have only one reading and be reduced to manipulating its own agenda in order to force its views on sometimes recalcitrant ministers. We need also to have majority voting in the Council of Ministers so that we are no longer in the situation where one difficult country can stop progress across the Community. Thirdly, I would like to see the Council meetings opened up to the gaze of people like you and me who actually put the members there. Is it such a very revolutionary thing that the Council of Ministers should at least publish their Minutes? Now I do realize that that is seen as heresy, and as some kind of horror vision of the future that they should actually be committed to publishing the Minutes of what they do, but at a time when Eastern Europe is democratizing it is quite unacceptable that with free elections all over the rest of Europe we should still be in a situation where, if the European Community were a country and applied for membership of the European Community, it would be refused on the grounds that it was not a democracy! That is no way to formulate an environment policy, and we need to abolish this notion of the Council suffering from twelve different kinds of tunnel vision and yet somehow or other running the Community without telling us how the decisions were made.

The EC faces numerous important environmental problems: clearly we are concerned about global warming; clearly we will continue to be concerned about water pollution; clearly we are going to be concerned about waste. Above all at the moment we are concerned about implementation and enforcement of existing policy. In conclusion, I want to emphasize that it is vital that at every level we stop playing silly games of pretending that we can solve by ourselves the problems that we face. The business of conservation, the business of pollution control, the business of resource management and the business of handing on a healthy planet to our successors demands cooperation at all levels: it is far too important to be left either to narrow nationalism or to 'Euro-colonialism'.

Questions and Answers

Q   Alison Clark (Shandwick Public Affairs)

If it is true that the ecological labelling legislation is to be proposed a
a Regulation rather than as a Directive, what are your views on the
precedent that this sets, since it will be quite a new thing for environ
mental legislation to override the democratic process by being a
Regulation?

A   There are two separate elements here: one is the idea of legislation
coming out as a Regulation, the other is the idea of it being dealt with
by regulatory committee; the two things are different. The distinction
between a Regulation and a Directive is that a Regulation (once it's
agreed by the Council of Ministers) comes into force immediately in
all member states without the member states' governments having to
do anything at all. The argument in favour of this item being a
Regulation is that, as in agricultural policy where a great deal is done
by regulation, the supposition is that if countries were left to adopt
different standards for ecological labelling, then in the light of the
Cassis de Dijon case and the absence of barriers to trade, you could end
up in some difficulty. That is probably the rationale for dealing with it
by Regulation. Whether my committee will accept that or not is
another matter, and I can't predict what they are going to say.[5] What I
find unacceptable about the proposal is the suggestion that the
standards by which products are to receive an 'ecological label' are to
be determined by what is called 'regulatory committee', which is
frankly the EC's own little personal affront to democracy, because it
vests power in a committee of national experts: somebody from the
UK, somebody from France, somebody from Italy sits round a table
making policy decisions; they are not accountable to anybody – not
to the Commission, not to the Parliament, they don't publish their
findings or their minutes. I wrote to the Director-General in charge of
environment policy, telling him that if this proposal in this form came
before the Parliament we would reject it – there is no way that my
committee would agree to a regulatory committee handling this
issue.[6]

Q   Brian Thomas (Tioxide Group)
How do you feel the conflict between the competition elements and
the environmental elements in Regulations will eventually be recon-
ciled?

A   The titanium dioxide proposals were a perfect example of the blind
use of competition policy prejudicing our view of the environment.
The theory behind it is contained in the Treaty: if you have two

countries, each producing a particular product, and that product is traded on the international market but the company in the first country is operating in a regime where there are very strict environmental controls and the company in the second country is subject to no such controls at all, then there will be externalities imposed on the first and not imposed on the second; there will therefore be a distortion of competition, and you will therefore need to harmonize regulations in order to even out the competition. In the case of the titanium dioxide plants, what happened was that because of the legal need of the Community to deal with it in this way, you got into the crazy situation in which a plant discharging into the warm, relatively tideless, waters of the Mediterranean was being treated the same as a company discharging into the cold waters of the North Sea, with a very high tidal range and a strong current. That again stems from the curious notion that the environment doesn't actually vary from place to place. Because the environment is now very firmly in the Treaties we now have an opportunity of looking at environment policy as environment policy. We are still I think in uncharted waters here. You can make some kind of predictions based on (for example) how the European Court dealt with the Danish problem of returnable bottles and cans and so on – that is to say, you have to obey the requirements of the Treaty on competition policy unless you can demonstrate that what you are doing is strictly environmental, and the Danes won that particular case. Everything is going to hang, however, on the extent to which you can prove that a departure from the rigours of the internal market legislation is justified on strict environmental grounds (or public health grounds, come to that). What would happen now if the titanium dioxide Directive were unleashed on us, I do not know.

Notes

1. R. Carson, *Silent Spring* (originally published by Houghton Mifflin, Boston, Mass., 1962. Published in UK by Penguin Books in association with Hamish Hamilton).
2. For full discussion of the issue, see D. H. Meadows et al, *Limits to Growth*, Universe Books, New York, 1972.
3. You will remember A. A. Milne's story about Tigger coming to the forest and having breakfast; he says at one point 'and with one loud "worrah, worrah, worrah, worrah", he jumped at the end of the table

cloth, pulled it to the ground, wrapped himself up in it three times rolled to the other end of the room and after a terrible struggle got his head into the daylight again and said cheerfully "Have I won?" ' There are several in Brussels who could play that part quite happily in the film version!

4.   The Inter-Governmental Conference will continue its deliberations throughout 1991.
5.   A meeting of the committee to discuss this was still pending in late February 1991.
6.   Following receipt of the letter, the Director-General changed the proposal to take into account the points raised.

Reference

Completing the Internal Market (June 1985) White Paper for the Commissioners to the European Council.

4 Environmental Enforcement

Gordon McCartney

Local authorities have had to take account of concerns about the environment in the same way that business has. Local electors (and businesses' customers) have become more aware of, and better informed about, environmental dangers since the Chernobyl disaster; this has been manifested in widespread concern about the threat to the ozone layer and global warming. More emphasis is being put on the **quality of life and services**; a measure of the public mood is the great increase in membership of environmental groups, both on the national and the local level, and the interest that is being taken in decisions affecting the environment.

Regulation and Enforcement

When an Association of District Councils' (ADC) Working Party looked at controlling the problems caused by pollution in 1989, it agreed that any policy on pollution should have regard to the fine balance between environmental problems, economics and employment. It is fair to say that of these factors, the environment has increased in importance, and that this is an inevitable consequence of pressure by the public. The government has recognized this; in the mid-1980s, its rhetoric stressed the overwhelming need for business to be freed from the burden of controls; the climate has changed very rapidly since then. Evidence of this can be seen in the 1990 White Paper on environmental policy, with its emphasis on higher standards and on measures to encourage prudent and efficient use of energy and natural resources.

One area where this process has had an effect is waste disposal; the government has provided the framework to enable local authorities to be more aggressive in their enforcement. One reason for a tighter regime is that in the past the private sector has exploited loopholes, which have now been closed. Stronger powers were also given to local authorities in the Environmental Protection Bill[1] to deal with air pollution, litter control and statutory nuisance.

Although they will inevitably play a leading part in any authority's environmental strategy, regulation and enforcement are not the only ways in which local councils can tackle environmental issues. In the same way as many businesses, authorities are reviewing every aspect of their operations and all the services that they provide with **environmental protection** in mind – from energy conservation measures in council housing, through staff health to the use of recycled paper and lead-free petrol in council vehicles. They are also working with others – voluntary and community groups and the private sector – to improve and conserve the local environment.

It should be added that in the field of environmental enforcement, local authorities are not only accountable to community charge and business rate payers, but also to the government and Parliament, both of which have not been slow to criticize authorities that have not used their powers to the full. It is clear that if local authorities do not effectively use the powers that have been given to them by recent legislation there will either be central intervention and direction of their use, or they will be taken away completely and vested in other bodies.

Local authorities have a wide range of regulatory and enforcement responsibilities and powers in areas that affect the environment:

- **Environmental health**: control of pollution, prevention of nuisance, noise, litter, health and safety at work, etc.
- **Planning**: development control and enforcement, conservation of the countryside (tree preservation, etc.) and of the built environment
- **Trading standards**: consumer safety, policing claims about products' 'environmental friendliness'.

There is also a multitude of local Acts of Parliament and bye-laws that may give particular authorities powers to deal with specific problems. General powers allow authorities to take legal action for the 'protection or promotion of their area'.

Enforcement does not only mean taking legal proceedings. The aim of enforcement action is to ensure **compliance with the law in the public interest**, and this can be achieved through giving advice, by persuasion or by other means, such as use of market signals. The government's 1990 White Paper makes it clear that the application of environmental standards by law has served the UK well, and that it will continue to be the foundation of pollution control, but that it can be expensive and may not always be the best (or most cost-effective) approach. It points to the importance of **market mechanisms** (see Chapter 1 above), including taxation and prices, which can be used to influence producers and consumers (and which can usually be implemented by central government). Effective environmental strategy requires that all available means be **considered** and **implemented** coherently by all the agencies involved, both central and local.

In most cases, prosecutions will be taken only as a last resort. Where action does have to be taken (and there are cases where there is no other way!), not only is anyone found to have broken the law punished, but the proceedings may be publicized, encouraging others to look again at their own practices. There may be ways of attracting publicity short of prosecution — Swansea, for example, photographs fly-tippers, and publishes the photographs in the local press. This publicity, and its educational effect, often has a proportionately greater effect than any court sentence, and it can be used to target a particular problem or a specific area.

Enforcement authorities are not inherently 'anti-business', but they do have both a duty to enforce the law and an obligation to respond to the same pressures from the public as businesses do. Local authorities do in the main try to work with local businesses, and many have assisted business in avoiding problems (an example being the seminars that many local authorities held on the COSHH (Control of Substances Hazardous to Health) Regulations. It is clear that a cared-for environment is of value not just for its own sake, but is also good for business — no company wants to have a shop or factory next to that of an irresponsible polluter. Care for the environment is also good public relations — in the widest sense of the term — and for business (the remarkable success of Body Shop is a good example). Local authorities have a duty to keep offenders up to standard.

The Local Authority's Enforcement Role

This has five aspects:

- **Accountability**: the government has on more than one occasion stressed that local pollution problems should be dealt with by those who are **locally accountable**. Local authorities are conspicuous locally, and are under the supervision of elected members who, although they will not interfere in particular cases, will set general policy and can be approached by business. Councils are invariably among the first bodies to which the public will turn in an emergency; their meetings are usually open, and they are now required to hold and display registers containing information on pollution, contaminated land, etc.
- **Local knowledge**: both councillors and enforcement officers will know the area concerned, its needs, customs and problems. They are able to respond **rapidly** to pollution incidents.
- **Ties with other local government functions**: local authorities have a range of relevant responsibilities: waste collection and disposal, highways, education and (perhaps most important) emergency planning, police and fire brigades.
- **Long experience**: local authorities have had enforcement powers over a very long period; indeed, the creation of the moden system of local government in the UK was to a great extent due to concern about environmental health. Structures such as the Local Authorities Coordinating Body on Trading Standards (LACOTS) have been set up in order to ensure that this expertise is shared.
- **Local authorities' coordinating role**: local authorities are well placed to coordinate action by other bodies, and can also act as a link between business and the local community.

Future Environmental Enforcement

The 1990 White Paper made it clear that there will be more enforcement in the future, and that the standards laid down will become more rigorous. The issue is still at the head of the political agenda and there are no signs that this is likely to change:

- The **White Paper** clearly indicated that it was the government's intention to strengthen the **anti-pollution regime**, with increased

powers to allow local authorities to act against those ignoring planning
requirements, new targets for air pollution, higher standards and tighter
controls on noise pollution and increased penalties for polluting water.

- The **Department of Trade and Industry** (DTI) has underlined this by
  telling business that 'The message is clear: as we move into the 1990s
  business will have to operate to significantly higher environmental
  standards than ever before'.[2]
- The **Environmental Protection Bill** added significant new requirements, and the expected planning bill will almost certainly tighten
  planning enforcement.
- There will also be wide-ranging environmental legislation from the
  European Community (EC) which has been considering measures on
  waste control, the regulation of biotechnology, limits on discharges
  into water, access to environmental information and environmental
  labelling of products (See Chapter 3).

How Will Enforcement Authorities Respond?

Already a great deal of thought is being given by local government to the
implications for all its activities and services on environmental policy. The
ADC considers that it is essential to maintain public confidence in the
regulatory system, while making it as accessible, comprehensible, flexible
and simple in operation as possible. In particular, any streamlining of the
regulatory process consistent with these aims and clarification of the
respective roles of local authorities and bodies such as HM Inspectorate of
Pollution (HMIP) would be welcome in order to avoid confusion to the
trade and to the public.

Possible developments in local government enforcement are:

- Extension of arrangements similar to LACOTS to **ensure consistency
  and sharing of expertise and information** between authorities: a
  major complaint of business is that local enforcement authorities'
  requirements and standards differ across the country; while this is to
  some extent inevitable because of the facts of each case and varying
  local circumstances (and the resources available to the authorities concerned), steps can be taken to reduce, as far as possible, differences in
  interpretation and **application** of the law. There are already a number
  of organization (such as the Local Authorities/Health and Safety Executive Liaison Committee, HELA or IPLA [Her Majesty's Inspectorate of
  Pollution/Local Authorities Enforcement Liaison Committee] set up

in conjunction with HMIP jointly established by central bodies and local government), which monitor enforcement and seek to deal with problems such as inconsistency. LACOTS was established by the local authority associations to help ensure uniformity in the administration and enforcement of the wide range of trading standards legislation.

Enforcement might also be made easier for all concerned by greater use of the 'home authority' principle used by LACOTS, whereby all action against a particular company is referred through the authority covering a **company's head office**. Joint working between authorities is essential to deal with environmental problems, which **do not respect local goverment boundaries**.

- Consideration of **new ways of organizing local authority inspectorates**: at present, different departments generally deal with each of an authority's regulatory functions. The establishment of multi-purpose inspectorates has been suggested by the Local Government Training Board (LGTB), unifying the different groups of inspectors employed by an authority. Such inspectorates would report to the different departments within an authority, but could be given a **general environmental remit**, allowing resources to be switched from one activity to another, according to local authorities.
- Consideration is also being given to **new emphases in enforcement**: local authorities are increasingly looking at **quality assurance** – whether a company has mechanisms and procedures to prevent pollution from occurring, how these are checked and maintained, etc.
- More **training for enforcement staff**: the LGTB document 'The Environmental Role of Local Government' (2), points out that:

> The environmental enforcement departments have not been conspicuous consumers of the local government management courses on offer. The enhanced importance of their role and its nature makes it increasingly important that they should participate more widely in management training, which, because of the fragmented nature of environmental concerns, must concentrate on inter-organisational relationships and group dynamics. Political sensitivity, the prioritisation of resources and strategic planning are skills that those concerned with the environment must acquire quickly.

Local authorities are re-evaluating the staff that they employ, and are keen to bring in new specialisms, including experience of industry. More environmental training for other local government staff – and for **councillors** – may also be necessary.

- Effective relations **between regulatory authorities**: above all, there will be a need for enforcement authorities and business to **work together**. The DTI has advised businesses of the importance of developing open and effective relations with the regulatory authorities. There are encouraging signs that this is beginning; industry is working with local authorities and HMIP in the compilation of guidance notes on methods of pollution control not entailing excessive costs – the backbone of the air pollution provisions of the Environmental Protection Bill.

What Will Enforcement Authorities Expect From Industry?

Having set out what industry can expect from local authorities, we should consider what will be expected of **industry** itself:

- An indication that they accept the new controls, and a willingness to show that they have appropriate **policies** to deal with new requirements; also, where necessary, a programme of **improvements**.
- A more cordial and open relationship with local government; greater **participation** in local affairs and assistance to local authorities in improving the environment, in the widest sense of the word.
- A 'proactive' approach to environmental matters, taking steps (perhaps in conjunction with the local authority) to **prevent problems from arising** rather than waiting for difficulties to occur. Most importantly, enforcement authorities should not be seen merely as 'policemen'. Problems can be avoided if difficulties are discussed as early as possible – during design or construction of a plant, for example. Authorities can (and do) give advice on new legislation, which may be of particular value at a time when major new environmental provisions can be expected.

On a national level, the CBI could include local authority representatives on some of its environmental policy bodies.

It is possible – and necessary – for business and enforcement authorities to work together to ensure a better environment for all.

Appendix 1   Principal Local Authority Environmental Enforcement Powers

Public Health Acts 1936 and 1961

- Notices requiring remedying of defective drainage, repair of blocked drains/private sewers, remedying leaking or overflowing cess pools and the provision of sanitary conveniences
- The control of statutory nuisances (e.g., premises, animals, noise, accumulations or deposits, dust or effluvia caused by a business, trade, etc. that are prejudicial to health or a nuisance
- The control of defective premises (those prejudicial to health or a nuisance)
- Control of certain 'offensive trades' (e.g., bone boilers, glue makers, soap boilers)
- The power to seek court orders requiring the closure or restriction of polluted water supplies.

Clean Air Act 1956 and 1968

- Enforcement of prohibition of dark smoke from chimneys and industrial and trade premises
- Control of emission of grit and dust from furnaces
- Approval of height of chimneys serving furnaces
- Control of smoke nuisances
- Enforcement of smoke control area restrictions.

Control of Pollution Act 1974

- Licensing of private waste disposal sites
- Control of noise nuisance.

Health and Safety at Work Act 1974

- Enforcement of health and safety at work legislation on certain premises (offices, shops, catering, hotels, etc.), including power to seize articles or substances on any premises causing imminent danger of serious personal injury.

Housing Acts

- Repair and clearance of houses unfit for human habitation, etc.
- Control of houses in multiple occupation (overcrowding, management orders, provision of amentities, etc.).

Food Safety Act 1990

- Control of food unfit for human consumption
- Power to examine and seize food
- Registration of food premises
- Licensing of slaughterhouses and knackers' yards
- Licensing of slaughtermen
- Registration of dairies and distributors of milk
- Powers to close food premises
- Control over unfit meat.

Town and Country Planning Act 1971

- Control of development
- Prevention of unauthorized development
- Conservation of the built heritage
- Tree preservation.

Consumer Protection Act 1987

- Prevention of sale of unsafe goods.

Environmental Protection Act 1990

- Responsibility for control of some seventy polluting processes (including timber processing, handling of cement, gas turbines and maggot breeding) covering an estimated 30 000 premises
- Control of litter
- Collection of supermarket trollies.

Appendix 2 Summary of Proposals in 1990 White Paper Affecting Local Government and Business

Aims

The White Paper has four main aims:

1. To **preserve** and **enhance** Britain's natural and cultural inheritance
2. To encourage the more **prudent** and **efficient use** of energy and other resources which global problems demand, and ensure that Britain meets its commitments for reducing global warming, ozone depletion and acid rain
3. To make sure that Britain's **air** and **water** are clean and safe, and that controls over wastes and pollution are maintained and strengthened where necessary
4. To maintain Britain's contribution to **environmental research** and encourage a better understanding of the environment, and a greater sense of responsibility for it, among everyone in Britain.

The White Paper gives the government's clear intention to strengthen the regime against polluters and to enhance the 'polluter pays' principle; the government does not feel, however, that this should be done by regulation alone. It has identified two broad approaches to controlling pollution and tackling environmental problems:

1. **Regulation**, in which standards or actions are applied by law
2. **Market signals**, including taxes and prices which can be used to influence producers and consumers.

The aim is to avoid pollution where possible and to ensure that those who cause environmental damage face the full cost of control (the 'polluter pays' principle), and thus have a clear incentive to act more responsibly.

The government believes that the regulatory approach has served Britain well in the past and will continue to be the foundation of pollution control, but it can be expensive and may not always deliver the most cost-effective solutions.

The White Paper is divided into 22 Chapters, a number of which will have implications for industry and its relationship with local authorities. The Chapter headings of relevance to district councils are set out below, with an indication of the action that is intended.

Land Use

In seeking to promote the best available use of land, the government will:

1. Make detailed **district level plans** compulsory
2. Enable local authorities to act more effectively against those who **ignore planning rules**
3. Make it easier for local authorities and developers to agree on ways to **protect** and **enhance** the environment as new development takes place
4. Look for further ways to improve the **environmental assessment** of new roads, and of other transport projects
5. Concentrate **derelict land funding** where it can do most to improve the local environment
6. Explore further ways of **preventing dereliction** and of bringing more vacant land back into **productive use**
7. Propose increased powers for local authorities over the siting and appearance of **new farm and forestry buildings**.

Towns and Cities

The government will:

1. Promote measures (including 'red routes' in London) to **civilize traffic in towns** and to reduce congestion through better traffic management and public transport, including providing bus priority schemes and sensible parking strategies

2. Provide **bypasses** where needed to relieve towns of through traffic, and study traffic management measures to maximize their benefits.

Air

The White Paper commits the government to new targets for air quality in Britain based on health and environmental needs. It will:

1. Base action increasingly on **air quality standards**, with advice from a new expert group
2. Extend and improve monitoring of **air pollution**
3. Press the EC for **tighter emissions standards** to control smoke from heavy diesels and for improved enforcement and testing
4. Press the EC for new Directives on toxic and dangerous waste **incineration**
5. Help to develop specifications for **less or non-polluting building products** in the EC
6. Provide new guidance against threats from **indoor pollution**, for example from radon gas
7. Strengthen existing controls and explore longer-term action against **legionnaires' disease**.

The government reaffirms its commitment to tackle long-range pollutants. It will:

1. Press for early EC agreements for new lorry standards to reduce **oxides of nitrogen emissions**
2. Work to control the volatile organic compounds which contribute to **ground-level ozone**
3. Work towards revised agreements internationally on **sulphur dioxide and oxides of nitrogen**
4. Support EC proposals for a Directive to control **ozone levels**

Noise

To improve standards and strengthen controls the government will:

1. Seek to tighten international noise regulations for **vehicles and aircraft**

2. Examine how barriers, design and better surfaces can make **road** quieter
3. Consider covering noise in the **MOT test**
4. Include noise in the **labelling of products**
5. Improve advice to local authorities on planning permission for **nois** (or **noise-sensitive**) **development**
6. Extend **noise insulation** schemes to limit exposure to noise from nev rail lines
7. Make it easier for local authorities to set up **noise control zones** and encourage consistent local authority practice on noise
8. Examine the need for further action on **helicopters** and **small airfield** and carry out research
9. Carry out research into **disturbance from aircraft** at night.

The government is considering further proposals for change from ar independent working group.

Water

The government will increase maximum fines for water pollution offences

Waste and Recycling

To encourage waste reduction the government will:

1. Press ahead with **Integrated Pollution Control** (IPC)
2. Widen its support for **clean technologies**
3. Work with local authorities to assess the effectiveness of **experimental recycling projects**
4. Encourage more **recycling 'banks'**, such as can, plastic and bottle banks
5. Work up a scheme for **labelling** recycled and recyclable products
6. Look for other ways of encouraging companies to recycle more **building materials** and **wastes from mining**; and to extract recyclable products from **domestic waste**.

Questions and Answers

Q   Barry Hyman (Marks & Spencer plc)
I don't see anything wrong, to use your own words, in local authorities being seen as a 'policeman' if you accept that the first job of the police is to prevent crime rather than to catch the criminal *post factum*. Do you think the local authority has enough power at the moment to do what it needs to do? If so, does it already use it effectively? If not, what other powers does it need?

A   The powers which local authorities have now and have had for some time are very extensive, and the Environmental Protection Bill will in fact impose upon local authorities considerably more powers and responsibilities. We know that there is likely to be a planning bill in the next parliamentary session and, given the thrust of the government's 1990 White Paper, more legislation will flow in due course, and if there were a change of government the process might well be accelerated. I would say that our powers are already extensive. We can argue about individual areas of activity where we might say we would like more power and you might argue to the contrary. Where I believe there is a problem is with resources. It's all very well giving local authorities powers, but if they haven't the resources to implement the legislation then the job becomes increasingly difficult. One of the problems about the Environmental Protection Bill is that very extensive new responsibilities are being placed upon authorities, but the resources are not likely to match the powers being assigned. One of the advantages of local authority involvement is that of course local authorities are free to review priorities, and you may well find that some authorities apply a higher priority to some kinds of enforcement action than others do. That may cause other problems, of course, for those who prefer to see a uniform system across the country. But the difficulty lies not with the powers but with the resources.

Q   Charles Miller (Public Policy Unit)
You stressed the need for business and local authority to form a closer partnership. You also referred to possible lack of local authority resources to carry out their new responsibilities under the Environmental Protection Bill. Do you have any specific examples of areas where we could usefully see business and local authority forming, say, co-ventures?

A   There already are a number of examples of local authorities and
businesses working together – guidelines on pollution, for instance.
But I do believe the local authority associations and bodies like the
CBI and their equivalent in specific industries could actually make
enormous strides if we could produce further codes of guidance
relating to the enforcement of specific legislation. There are going to
be a number of areas in the field of pollution, a whole range of
problems relating to waste disposal. My own association published in
1988 two very important papers on the problems of pollution control
and the disposal of hazardous waste; there are areas in those two fields
where through the national bodies you could get dialogue between
both sides of the table, with industry and local authority working
together. I really do believe that the emphasis in the future is going to
be on working to an agreed code in many different areas, whether it's
in relation to pollution, to food safety, the whole range. I earnestly
hope that we can get that kind of machinery moving between national
bodies in business and in local government, and in the local community as well. Some of you may well already be party to local dialogue
but I cannot emphasize too greatly the importance of it. Where there
are plants and processes actually on the ground in towns and cities the
opportunity for building good relationships, for laying down procedures for dealing with emergencies, future government policies and
so on, is enormous. That's where I would have to see our emphasis in
the future.

Q   Samuel Radcliffe (British Cast Metals' Industry Research Association)
The tradition of pollution control has been one of cooperation
between industry and local authority, and particularly in the area
where my own industry is strongest, the West Midlands. But we have
been involved directly with the local authority representatives and
HMIP in discussing guidance notes to follow up the Environmental
Protection Bill on pollution control from our industry. One of the
things I have found surprising is that the driving force for the
emergence of these guidance notes which the Secretary of State will
be issuing is a political agenda in the Environment Department in
central government. I have asked what account is taken of the corresponding economic cost of it – whether they talked to the Department
of Industry, for instance – and I have found that there is no mechanism
within central government for this dialogue to take place. I am
concerned that there is no place where this isssue is examined in the
round.

A   It's an open secret that government departments have not seen eye to eye on environmental policy – there has, for instance, been a conflict between Environment and Transport on the future role of the motor car, and we know that this has been the subject of lively exchanges between other government departments. But the White Paper now represents long-term government strategy, and it's the blueprint we must work to. There are many examples of cooperation between local government and the private sector, particularly in the field of pollution control. I acknowledge that, and I think that there are areas in the future – as environmental issues become more and more sensitive within the community at large – where there will have to be new approaches. If, for example, the government is going to legislate to get rid of CFCs, how do we dispose of old refrigerators? Some of you may be actively involved in local initiatives here, and this is the kind of area where change in environmental policy will lead to a sudden upsurge in demand for local services. There may be changes in your production activities which have an impact on the community, either with regard to the disposal of waste or the imposition of tighter controls over noise or smell. Where good relations already exist they must be the basis of closer cooperation. Where they are not so good, we must work harder to make them better.

Q   Hugh Billot (Sheerness Steel Company plc)
Many UK companies are very conscious of the environment and keen to work with local authorities to solve the common problems. But what about where the problems are well known, but the cures are not so well known, and companies have to be involved in leading-edge technology to try and overcome them – which takes a great deal of capital and also time?

A   This is a very important point. A burden is placed on industry as it seeks to find new ways of dealing with a problem which has environmental implications; that can involve expense. At the same time national and local government, perhaps being the cause of those problems, is also anxious to help industry find the right solution. I believe that national and local government and the private sector have to work together in that research field as well. I don't know what plans the government has to assist with that; I expect they will say, as they have said before, it is for the private sector to fund its own research. But I know that in local government there is deep concern that more needs to be done to help industry to find solutions which benefit the community as a whole. We certainly want to explore the opportunity of joint research activity between public and private sector to achieve what we all want – and that is a better environment.

Notes

1. Which received the Royal Assent on 1 November 1990; most of the Environmental Protection Act's provisions came into force on 1 January 1991.
2. 'The Environmental Role of Local Government' (1990) (London, LGTB).

References

This Common Inheritance (1990) Cmd 1200 (London, HMSO).
Nuclear Waste and Radiation Risks (1988) (London, ADC).
Pollution: Controlling the Problems (1988) (London, ADC).

5 Anticipating Consumer Trends

Jeff Fergus

Anticipating consumer trends in 'green-ness' is no easier than in any other type of forecasting – in fact, you might say that in this case we're dealing with a particularly 'foggy' crystal ball, with more than its fair share of unknowable and uncontrollable variables clouding our 'vision'. In marketing-speak, I suppose we ought to be describing our forecasting activities not as 'blue-sky-ing' but more as 'very-hazy-grey-sky-ing'!

But whatever our forecasting technique, it is abundantly clear – and indeed the speakers in this conference leave no room for doubt – that 'green' issues or environmental concerns *are* going to have a huge impact on every facet of our lives, especially as many of us are in the position of making decisions about green issues in the course of our working lives that could potentially shape the domestic lives of millions of people, both here and abroad. This chapter consists of three parts. The first poses the question 'How will "green consumerism" evolve?', a question on the lips of all interested parties in this debate. The second looks at **tracking and forecasting**. I don't pretend to have the answers at my fingertips – my personal crystal ball has as many problems as everyone else's. However, carefully designed **tracking studies** can help us tease out clues to the **future** by building up a detailed picture of the **past** – and the direction and pace of **change**. Only by tracking or monitoring trends in relevant attitudes and behaviour, over a period of time, can we afford to indulge in – and act in response to – the risky business of **forecasting**.

The third part touches on advertising – which, as a powerful **effector** o change as well as a **reflector** of shifts in societal mores and values – wil have a key role to play in the shaping of 'green' things to come. M objective is to contribute to and facilitate decision-making processes by introducing a new slant on corporate environmental activities, and by making recommendations for immediate consideration at corporate level.

Before hypothesizing about how 'green consumerism' is likely to evolve it will help to define our terms. First, what are we really talking about wher we use the term 'green consumerism'? Secondly, how does this 'greer consumerism' manifest itself: is it an 'all or nothing' state, or are there discrete, and identifiable, stages between the pale pastel greens and the darl tones of full-bodied green commitment? And, thirdly, what are the lessons from overseas? If we look beyond national boundaries to developments ir other countries and cultures, we can gain valuable insights into the deve lopment of 'green consumerism' – here, perhaps, is a way to impose order on this vast and somewhat daunting subject.

'Green Consumerism'

A few years ago, the phrase 'green consumerism' might have conjured up images of pressure groups taking up the cause whilst the rest of us stood by the sidelines and, to be honest, didn't really give a fig – let alone an organically grown one. But in the 1990s, 'green consumerism' has a very different connotation. Nowadays it refers as much to the **individual consumer**, for whom 'green' concerns are not in any way 'cranky' or 'fringe', but are an increasingly important part of their everyday lives. I have therefore assumed a definition of 'green consumerism' which centres on the individual: 'interest in, purchase of, and agitation for "green" or "greener" products by individual consumers'.

'Green Consumerism' in Action

It would be naively optimistic, and somewhat inaccurate, to assume that – once aware of green issues – greens are individually organizing petitions, boycotting manufacturers and retailers and actively promoting 'the cause' in the interests of the planet. More accurately, there appears to be a 'gradient' of green opinion and action. Figure 5.1 demonstrates development from a superficial awareness of such global issues as holes in the ozone layer and acid rain, into *personal* concern about those issues, which

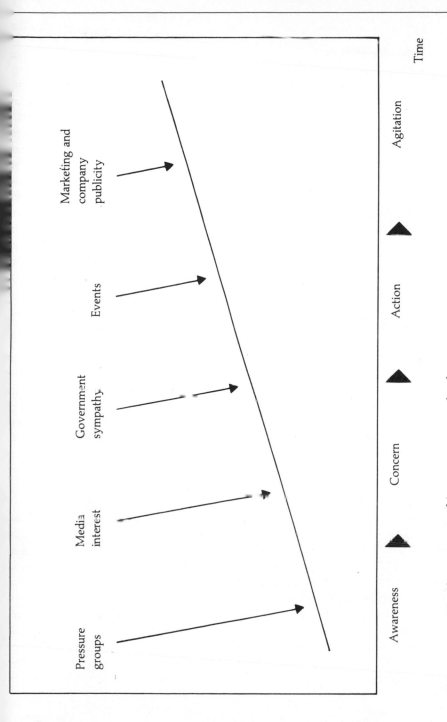

Figure 5.1 The four stages of 'green consumerism'

then translates into *action* – buying ozone-friendly aerosols, for example, o
unbleached toilet paper. Ultimately this is the link to 'agitation' – writing to
MPs, joining Greenpeace or Friends of the Earth.

The nature and pace of this development is interwoven with the
influences upon it – such as media coverage, government reports, news o.
environmental accidents or scandals and manufacturers' messages. Interest
ingly, this same gradient can be applied to **international comparisons** o
'greenness': in a European context, Italy (for example) is at the 'awareness
stage of green consumerism, while Germany is the master of 'agitation'.

Lessons From Overseas

Pursuing this point, what can we learn from taking an **international** view?
Green thinking has some 'epicentres' – for instance, West Germany and
parts of Scandinavia (where the environment has been at the centre of
political debate since the early 1980s) and the North-East and West of the
United States (where the solid waste crisis is of mounting concern). Looking
at the data available to us on consumer opinion and behaviour in Europe
and the USA, it is interesting to note that the development of 'green
consumerism' on a national basis appears to be, in part, a function of
proximity to these epicentres: the farther away from the 'eye', the less
interest and the less action is seen. This observation applies broadly to
government as well as to **consumer action**.

In terms of sheer numbers of directives and measures adopted by
governments to encourage 'greener' behaviour, Finland, Sweden and West
Germany demonstrate relatively high levels of overt action in the form of
charges, taxes and subsidies, while Italy (and, surprisingly, Belgium) are
some way behind. Whilst we may think of Western Europe as being
greener than the USA, it, too, is ahead of most of the rest of Europe.

Our 'epicentre' observation throws up some other interesting facts and
figures. In Europe, penetration and availability of lead-free petrol highlights
the chasm between Germany on the one hand and Spain on the other (see
Figure 5.2). And if we look at relative prices across the Continent, taking
the index figure of unleaded petrol over leaded four-star, a similar gradient
emerges: broadly (as Figure 5.3 shows), the further south you go, the lower
the unleaded cost benefit. In Spain, drivers are penalized for going 'green'!

So far, we've been looking to Europe, and might logically assume that
green awareness and thinking emanate from Scandinavia, and (in particular)
West Germany. If we delve into our respective rubbish heaps, however,
Europe (and especially the UK) has much to learn from the USA. In kg per

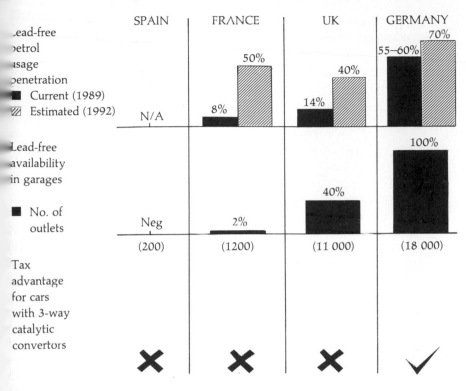

Figure 5.2   'Greenness' in the garage

person per day, the amount of 'garbage' produced by the USA is probably the highest in the world, and therefore methods for its disposal have for some time been fighting their way up the agenda of green priorities. British waste output *per capita* is not far behind that of the USA. The population of the States is becoming increasingly aware and concerned about the problems that too much rubbish creates – why not the British? Disposal of household garbage and decreasing space in what the Americans call 'landfill sites' are issues that concern the American populace as much as the ozone layer and acid rain, as Figure 5.4 demonstrates. In the UK, they don't even warrant a mention (see Figure 5.5). We assume that once the bin or bag is outside the front door, it no longer exists. It is also remarkable to note the significant differences in levels of concern about **other issues** – according to these particular studies, the average British consumer is apparently far less bothered than his or her American counterpart about a variety of global issues. The role of the media in influencing attitudes on waste

Figure 5.3   Relative prices of unleaded petrol, Europe

	UK (%)	USA (%)
• Ozone layer	87	92
• Car exhaust pollution	84	90
• Air pollution	81	90
• Acid rain	82	85
• Decreasing space in landfill sites	N/A	**90**
• Disposal of household garbage	N/A	**86**

Figure 5.4   Awareness of selected environmental issues, UK and USA

	UK (%)	USA (%)
• Toxic waste	N/A	**77**
• Air pollution	19	70
• Ozone layer	47	67
• Car exhaust pollution	25	60
• Acid rain	8	55
• Decreasing space in landfill sites	N/A	**53**
• Disposal of household garbage	N/A	**48**

Figure 5.5   Concern about selected environmental issues, UK and USA

disposal in the UK in the next few years will be interesting to observe. From our experience of qualitative work at Leo Burnett UK, we have become increasingly aware of spontaneous consumer concern about **over-packaging** and **waste** – even the size of teabags has come under fire for being a waste of paper – so although we have a long way to go, waste disposal is likely to become a high-profile topic in the near future.

A point I shall elaborate upon later is the growing interest not just in products and their packaging, but in the **environmental performance of manufacturing companies**. A survey undertaken by the Diagnostics company on behalf of *Marketing* magazine revealed that respondents had very clear images of the 'do-gooders' and the 'wrong-doers': if I tell you that these particular respondents were all marketing professionals you may be tempted to reappraise the results, if not dismiss them, but a 1989 study on consumer 'greenness' by Leo Burnett (see Figure 5.6) produced consistent findings in terms of company 'rating' – after all, marketing professionals are consumers, too, and all consumers are closet marketing professionals, as we all know!

What can other countries' experience tell us about how 'green consumerism' is likely to evolve? Broadly, four trends seem to be emerging.

First, in countries like the UK, a gradual move towards **more widespread agitation**. As the German example shows, power will increasingly lie in the hands of the consumer. According to *Marketing*, the demand for whole markets could drop as they become unpopular, or as prices are forced up through green legislation. For example, intense consumer pressure in Germany has contributed significantly to the demise of the 'Tetrapak' carton in the soft drinks sector, in favour of good old returnable glass bottles. In the UK, much consumer 'action' to date has followed manufacturer leads (e.g., purchasing unbleached toilet paper once it had been made available) but this will change as 'green' ideas spread into all sectors of the

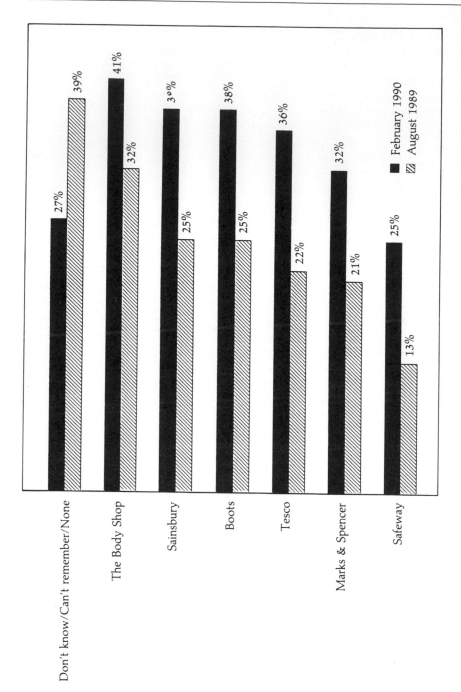

Figure 5.6   Awareness of UK stores believed to be helping protect the environment

population, not just the young and educated, and as we all become more vocal about our concerns.

Secondly, we will see a consumer interest not only in the 'green' credentials of products, but also in their **packaging and production**. In the USA, considerable emphasis is being placed on the development of better waste management and recycling programmes in the bid to ease pressure on landfill space; in California (one of the 'epicentres' for new 'green' thinking), the development of clean production technology is a priority for investment. In Germany (and more and more elsewhere, as we've seen), environment-friendly packaging is no longer enough – *over*packaging is also under fire from the impatient green consumer, who can distinguish between what is functional and what is not.

Thirdly, the development of a public opinion climate which favours legislation rather than voluntarism. Even in Germany, where (as Figure 5.2 demonstrated) the level of government action is relatively high, the government is still not thought to be tough enough. This change from a 'piecemeal' to a *'holistic'* view refers to the development of a deeper consumer understanding of the **wider ecological effects** of individual pieces of consumption and the real environmental costs – not just of consuming or using a particular product, but of that producer's production, packaging and disposal. With this new awareness will come a parallel shift of emphasis from 'consumption' (the hallmark of the 1980s) to 'conservation'. Individual responsibility will extend beyond the simple inclusion of 'green' products in the weekly shop to encompass a raft of recycling and energy-saving activities which call for personal and active involvement.

Finally the growing normalization of 'green' formulated products will gradually render **'green' product edges** less marketable, so the focus of 'green' marketing will switch to the **company level**: good corporate environmental performance will become an integral aspect of total quality. At the same time, consumers will become **less prepared** to accept green products which involve a **trade-off** or **compromise** on any current benefit – a reinterpretation of 'green' as an additional benefit of the products and brands they are accustomed to using, and which they will increasingly come to expect. This leads us on to consider the role of **tracking** in forecasting the future of 'green' concerns.

Corporate Strategy

From the point of view of business and the formulation of future strategy, an internationally open view on events, *plus* a survey approach to monitor-

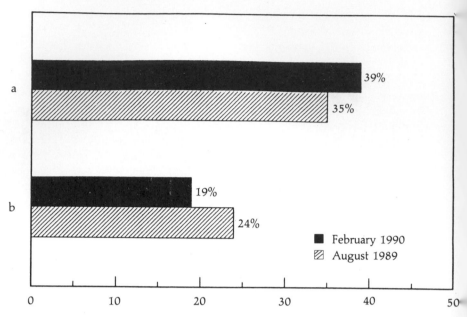

a   I buy Green alternatives as long as they don't cost too much more than other products
b   I never consider the issue of Green alternatives when I'm shopping

Figure 5.7   UK attitudes to alternative 'green' products when shopping

ing opinion over time, can bring more confidence in looking to the future. Monitoring opinion will 'flesh out' observations and hypotheses and lend quantitative weight to planning decisions. Clearly, the earlier tracking studies are set in motion, the better, because the earlier the company will feel confident about the trends demonstrated and the decisions that need to be made.

Opinion is moving quite rapidly and, even at six-month intervals, significant change can be discerned. Leo Burnett in both the UK and the USA have been involved in tracking different facets of green attitudes and behaviour, and the speed with which consumer opinion moves can be surprising. Figures 5.7–5.10 show the kind of changes that have taken place: green consumerism will not only affect our personal lives, it will also demand changes in **corporate policy**. Here are a few suggestions for how a company can capitalize on this marketing opportunity.

• First, start **monitoring** consumer attitudes and behaviour **as soon as**

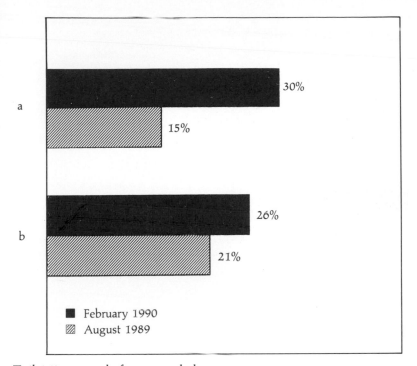

a Toilet tissue made from recycled paper
b Unleaded petrol

Figure 5.8 Environmentally friendly products bought/owned, UK

possible!

- Secondly, consider seriously the possibility of forming a **multi-disciplinary team**, representative of all departments to plan **environmental policy**, allocating to one individual the responsibility for monitoring attitudes to green issues on an ongoing basis. This member of the team will keep you up-to-date with market developments, not only in your own market, but in **related markets here and abroad**.

- Finally, right from the start, it is worth making sure that, as well as monitoring the general development of 'green consumerism', you measure the **reputation of your own company**. If you haven't already taken steps to do so, now is the time to embark on a reexamination of every aspect of your operation from a 'green' perspective. A **positive corporate image** on environmental matters is set to become increasingly important (see Chapter 8).

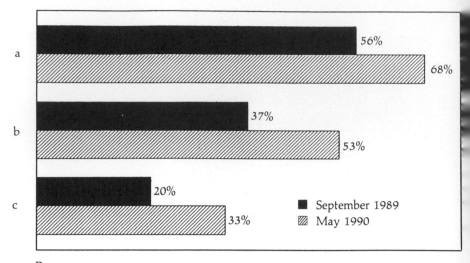

a   Papers
b   Glass bottles
c   Plastics

Figure 5.9   Those claiming to save/separate for recycling, USA

Our survey checklist (Figure 5.11) highlights areas for inclusion on your 'green' research agenda.

'Green Advertising'

This leads us into the final part of my chapter: the role of advertising. Again, if we take a step back and look at what has gone **before**, we can pick up clues as to how the potential of advertising – as a very powerful opinion former – might best be exploited in the **future** from a manufacturing (or retailing or service) company perspective.

First of all, then, let us consider the **context** in which 'advertising with a green slant' will be operating. We've already seen some quite hard-hitting advertising from **pressure groups**, and this is likely to continue, heating up the climate of public opinion.

Second, it is important to acknowledge that consumers are increasingly **sceptical** of what they see as manufacturers jumping on a 'green bandwagon'. As *Marketing* pointed out in 1990:[1]

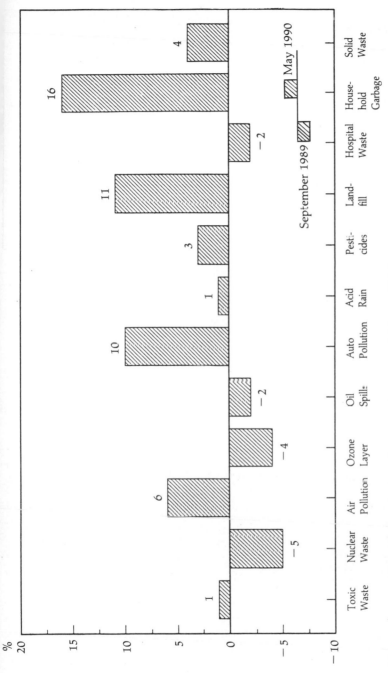

Figure 5.10 Change in concern about environmental issues, USA

NB. This chart shows 'plus' and 'minus' changes in levels of concern about specific green issues in 1990 versus 1989 ie. 16 per cent more respondents cite household garbage as an area that concerns them in 1990 versus 1989, while 4 per cent less cite the ozone layer.

- Awareness of 'green issues'
- Level of concern
- Attitudes towards packaging
- Attitudes towards recycling
- Purchase of 'green' products
- Involvement in recycling, etc.
- Company images in your markets
- How 'green' is your company?

Figure 5.11   'Green' research agenda: corporate checklist

Consumer suspicion of big business is already being fuelled by allegations that many of the new 'environmentally friendly' products are only as green as the ink on their logos.

Vague or spurious product claims will fail to impress the green-literate consumer, and there is the very real danger of generating a nasty backlash. The Advertising Standards Authority in 1989 set up a new category for complaints about green advertising, in response to the growing consumer belief that marketers could not be trusted to be **honest** about their green credentials.

Third, in a similar vein, **regulatory guidelines** on the making of 'green claims' are being tightened, and strict **labelling codes** are likely to be introduced on a national – if not international – scale (see Chapter 4 above).

Fourth, green products – currently the exception rather than the rule in the vast majority of households – will come to be increasingly 'normal' and **unexceptional**. Because of this 'normalization' of green, we will need to think again about the motivational value and validity of green 'product edges' for brands in our respective portfolios and how the consumer is likely to respond. It is likely that when green claims are made in **product advertising**, they will increasingly have to be both **tangible** and **significant**, and inevitably over time, the role of advertising will shift towards the promotion of **corporate** 'greenness'.

Questions and Answers

Q   David Gilliatt (paper industry)
    We as an industry are just beginning to move into the 'green product' world: how can advertising help us project our message? And if we decide that the message that we want to give is one that is solely

concerned with our products, how do you as advisers make a judgement on whether the message you're putting across is factual, or just the one that the company wants you to give?

A   This is where your advisers will have to be very honest indeed. Any attempt to present what you would like people to think of you based on information that can later be shown to be erroneous will have a net effect infinitely worse than if you had not done anything at all. In the work that my own company has been involved in with some of our clients, we have been at enormous pains to discuss with their technical departments (not just in the UK but on a world-wide basis) the substantiation for the data, and to determine how we would explain exactly how the claims have been substantiated. Any advisers whom you do consult should test you rigorously on the substantiation which they are asked to put forward: to do anything else risks making the whole thing less than fully productive – and indeed, could make it counter-productive.

Notes

1.   'Green About Green', *Marketing* (September 24, 1990) pp. 28–35.

6 Corporate Responsibility

John Wybrew

From the standpoint of the oil industry we can forsee potentially more profound changes arising over the next ten–twenty years than we have seen in the previous fifty. These are the really profound changes resulting from the global concerns for the environment. Oil supplies something like 45 per cent of the world's energy requirements; it is substantially the most traded commodity in the world – which, of course, means that very large quantities of oil are moved by tanker and by pipeline around the world and across the oceans. Oil is a material unlike (say) gas or coal, which first of all has to undergo complex processing and refining (or maybe petrochemical processing) before it is available to the consumer in the form of end products, and there is no doubt at all that the oil industry for many years (perhaps since the start) has been at the forefront of concern about its **environmental impact**. I would like to believe that the major oil companies have been both conscious of that fact and extremely active in trying to **recognize** and **manage** the risks, based on current awareness of technology, of the environmental concerns, ecological impact, and so on.

We need to consider the management of the environment from the oil company point of view at three quite different levels. First of all the top level – the impact of **our operations** on the environment: movement of oil by tankers and pipeline, refineries, petrochemical complexes and the impact of those operations on the environment. Then, of course, there is the continuous impact of the uses of oil products, petrochemicals (and gas and

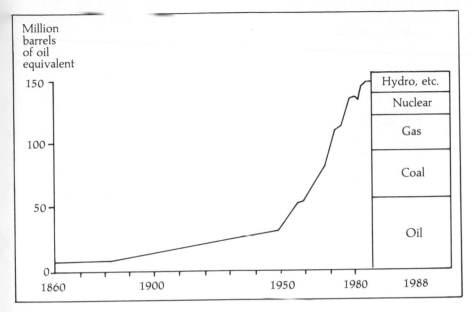

Figure 6.1   Global commercial energy demand

coal, for that matter) on the environment as they are used by **consumers**: the impact of leaded or unleaded petrol, and so on. This tends to be for the most part a **local** and **regional** impact but – and this is the feature which is novel in today's circumstances – there is the growing awareness of the big concerns about the **global environment**, particularly global warming or an augmented greenhouse effect, and the depletion of the ozone layer. It is these major concerns, which have surfaced since 1985, that are the ones with potentially the most profound implications for our industry.

Oil and the Environment

Figure 6.1 shows the build-up in the world's consumption of energy going back to the mid-nineteenth century through to the present time; since 1945 there has been a quite remarkable fivefold increase in the consumption of energy – which, of course, has accompanied the equally remarkable development of the world economy over the period since 1945. Something like 80 per cent of that energy is supplied in the form of **fossil fuels** – gas, goal and (something like 45 per cent of it) in the form of oil. And, of course, it is that linkage between economic growth and the dependence of economic growth on fossil fuels, and the impact of those fossil fuels when burnt, that is at the heart of the present dilemma about the global environment.

Accompanying that increase in our dependence on fossil fuel associated with economic growth, and that fivefold increase in the consumption of energy (much of it fossil fuel), has been an equally rapid build-up in **emissions of carbon dioxide** (CO_2) as a result of economic activity (see Figure 6.2). Coal is an important component – roughly 100 units of CO_2 are generated from (say) 1 unit of coal as against 70 per cent from oil and 50 per cent from natural gas – simply because coal is the most carbon-rich of the fossil fuels.

Is it possible to break the fundamental linkage with economic development, dependence on fossil fuels and the impact of fossil fuels when used on the environment? There is, in a sense, an encouraging pointer here because I doubt whether anyone who has not worked in the oil industry is quite so aware of the nature of the so-called 'oil shocks', by which we mean the two increases of oil prices (one occurring in 1973 and the other in 1977–9). Expressed in real terms, again going back to the mid-nineteenth century, we can see that the price of oil over much of that period was hovering around $10 a barrel; Figure 6.3 shows the consequence of the two major very large oil price increases. This was a quite unprecedented shock to the system, and what it did was break the seemingly irreversible link between economic growth and dependence on fossil fuels, at least in the advanced industrial countries. Consumers were jolted into an awareness of the sharp increase in the cost of oil and the advanced industrial countries changed their patterns of usage of energy, looked for more energy-efficient processes and introduced a whole range of measures to reduce the intensity of energy usage in the economy. Figure 6.4 shows the quite significant impact of that. The same challenge also arises today – not so much concerned with questions of the finite nature of oil reserves but more about the environmental impact of energy use.

Figure 6.5 shows the projected growth of the world's population. Much of it is almost predestined, it has a remorseless momentum about it: at present, we are around the 5 billion people mark, and on all normal projections within about thirty years we will be at around the 8 billion mark. The growth will take place not in the advanced industrialized countries (North America, Europe and so on), but in Asia, Africa and South America.

There is a dilemma. In Figure 6.6 we can see that units of consumption *per capita* of energy in the USA are already something like twice the consumption of Western Europe and considerably more than the less developed countries (LDCs) and yet all the growth in the world's popula-

CO₂
emissions
(gigatons C)

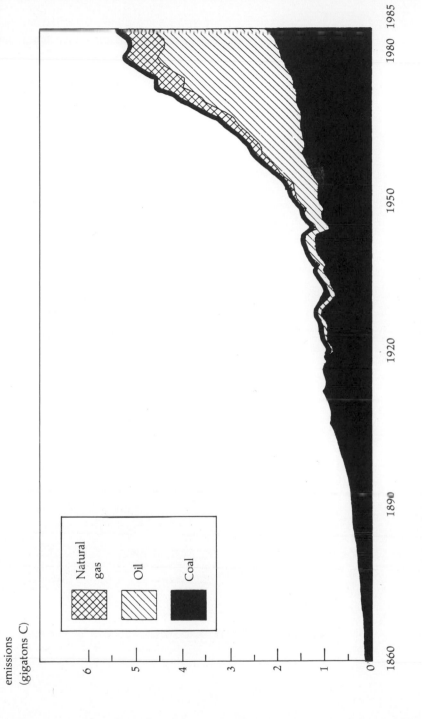

Figure 6.2   CO₂ emissions due to fossil fuel consumption, 1860–1985

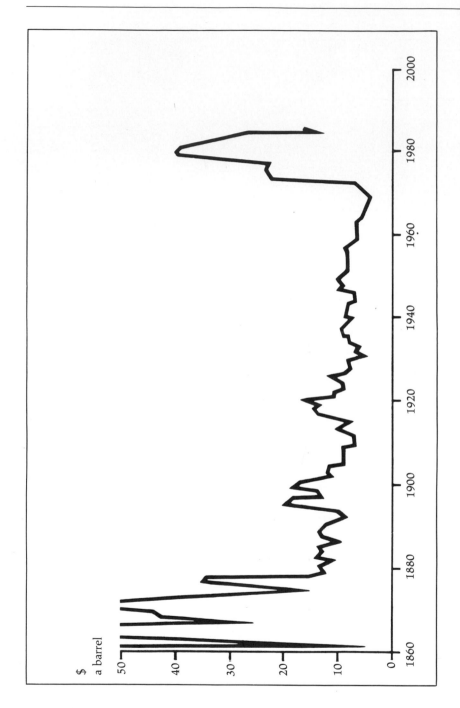

Figure 6.3   Historic crude oil prices

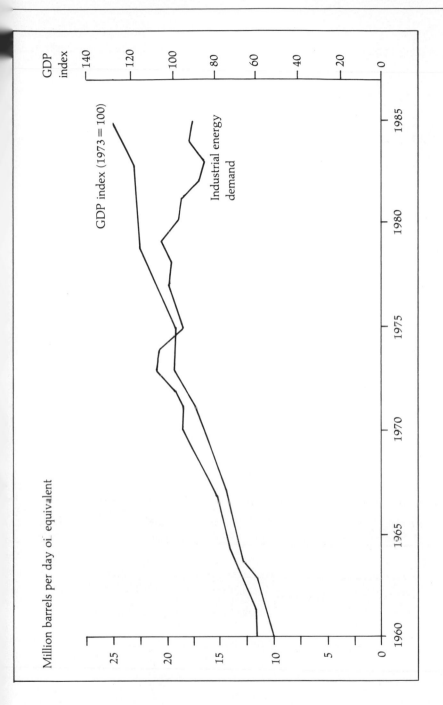

Figure 6.4   Industrial energy demand, OECD countries

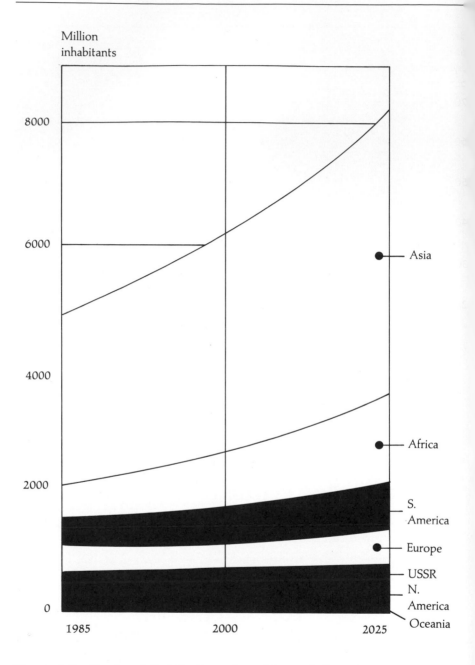

Figure 6.5   Regional distribution of world population

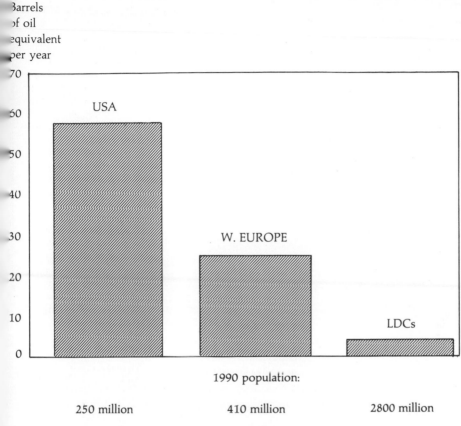

Barrels
of oil
equivalent
per year

Figure 6.6   *Per capita* consumption of primary energy

tion is projected to take place in LDCs, who naturally aspire to development and with it a call on the world's resources of fossil fuels, and with that
an inevitable impact on the environment. So it may be comforting in a
sense to look back at the impact of the oil shocks in the mid-1970s and
suggest that they at least broke the trend of continued growth in energy
consumption and energy intensity in the advanced countries. But when we
consider how small is energy use in the underdeveloped countries and look
at the burgeoning population forecasts, I think you can see something of
the challenge that lies ahead.

The key to solving the problem has to lie in greater **efficiency in the
supply and consumption usage** of energy, at all stages in the process. As
of today, without any change in the economic framework in which we

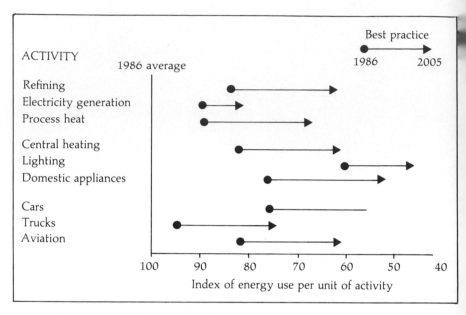

Figure 6.7   Potential energy efficiency improvements, OECD countries

operate, we could be saving 20 per cent. In Figure 6.7, we see the potential for increasing energy efficiency on a twenty-year time scale for a number of different typical processes – refining, electricity generation, lighting and central heating. You can see in all cases (and this is not anticipating great leaps of technology, but fairly steady improvements in technology, materials, information and so on) a potential for something like a 30 per cent improvement in the efficiency and application of energy.

Twenty per cent immediately, with 30 per cent potentially available with advancing technology: being more specific about the transportation sector (which is, of course, one in which we are deeply involved in the oil industry) the miles per gallon average of existing cars is currently something less than 30. The average new car coming onto the road is doing something in excess of 30 mpg – 32 or 33 would be typical. Volkswagen have prototypes (a combination of diesel and electric) capable of doing in excess of 100 mpg.

Just to illustrate the potential for advancing technology, I will mention one particular scheme which Shell sponsors each year called the Mileage Marathon. This is not an exercise in trying to make cars go faster, accelerating faster: it is based on the simple notion of producing a vehicle carrying at least one person and seeing how far such a vehicle can go on one gallon of petrol. These vehicles trundle along at 2 or 3 miles an hour (like sewing machines on wheels), but the record – 6400 mpg – is currently held by one made by Honda. This illustrates the enormous potential of technology which can be unlocked with the right sort of encouragement and the right sort of **economic framework**, and this is the challenge to all of us posed by CO_2 in the atmosphere. We can attempt to model the impact of CO_2 emissions growth on the global climate, but such models are very complex and can produce a wide variance of outcomes. We do not yet have conclusive evidence of the consequences of the phenomenon that we can observe; nonetheless there is no doubt that the potential dangers are so great that any responsible person would argue that we should take all sensible precautionary measures as of now, **ahead of that knowledge**.

In trying to set about this systematic process of improvement, we have constantly to be conscious of the resource **costs** and the **benefits** that we are seeking to achieve; it is so easy to pour enormous sums of money into this area, and the last thing we want to do is base it on **emotion** rather than **fact**. The principle of 'glasnost' – of an open debate, of a general consciousness of the problems and the solutions and the nature of the task that faces us – is essential (and, given the global nature of the problem so indeed is international cooperation, as distinct from any unilateral action that individual countries can take). The market has a part to play, but so too does regulation, and so too does information and exhortation.

Shell is comfortable with the founding principles on which the 1990 White Paper rests, and is wholly committed to the concept of 'sustainable development' (or, at least, progressive systematic responsible progress towards it, because this is not something which is achievable in a short space of time).

'Greener' Products

The development of consumer awareness of 'greener' products – and again I stress that I am looking at this from an oil company point of view – means that there is no merit in attempting to see this as a cosmetic exercise. Such pressures are reflected in the current research towards the elimination of lead in petrol; the reduction in lead levels in leaded petrol; the reduction in the vapour pressure of petrol so that less of it evaporates and goes into the environment; the reduction of sulphur, the reduction of benzene, etc. Each one of these can be achieved only by enormous investment on behalf of the world's refining industry. One of the reasons that the prices of oil products shot up as fast as they did at the time when Iraq moved into Kuwait in late

1990 was that for the first time in well over a decade the world's refining industry was pretty heavily loaded and it was having difficulty meeting the advancing environmental standards which had been set in the USA, across Europe, and in places like Japan.

Governments collectively have a part to play in setting **minimum standards**, and discussion and debate continues within Europe and the USA on the setting of minimum standards for the quality of oil products in areas like sulphur and lead content, etc. We are already seeing companies (conscious of the growing awareness of the public on environmental matters) seeing **commercial opportunity** as a driving force in encouraging them to move ahead to actually produce something which is more appealing to the customer based on differentiation on environmental quality – 'greener' products (see Chapter 5).

The question of **managing risk** is crucial. There is a tendency for the public to believe that all one needs to do is to urge the oil industry to clean up its act, and that will be sufficient to make it happen. In fact, changes in standards and improvements in quality (essential as they are) will necessarily be accompanied by considerable increases in **cost**. All the time, one is striving to manage those costs, to manage the risks, to make the trade-offs in a rational way to try to ensure that the resource cost and the consequences in price are commensurate with the benefits: it is very easy to spend large sums of money and not yield commensurate benefits.

Another vital principle is not to look at one narrow part of the process in which energy is produced, supplied, or consumed, without looking at the **entire cycle**, and the impact on the environment at **each stage** in that cycle and the **waste products** that result from it. A graphic example is the electric car. There is nothing wrong with the concept of the electric car; we may well see them being used in congested city centres and it is easy to think of the electric car with zero emissions or effectively zero emissions in places like London and say 'wonderful benefit to the environment'; but you can't ignore the environmental impact of the electricity, which has to be **generated** to provide **energy** for the car. When you move into the world of petrochemicals, you have equally to be concerned not just with the immediate **application** of the product, but with its **production**, the cost of producing it, the impact of production process, the **storage**, the application by the farmer or whoever, the subsequent effects of waste, and so on. There is an **entire chain of actions**, and each one has to be followed through. This is the concept of **product stewardship** – the responsibility of the company for the process from the very start, when a product is born right the way through to when the waste products are responsibly handled and dealt with. You cannot look only at a narrow part of it.

mpact of Operations

We must next consider the impact of oil company operations on the environment. Committees within Shell have been established to look at the question of what sort of **objectives** we should be setting for ourselves. What sort of expression should we give to the concept of 'sustainable development'; how can we reconcile our operations of sustainable development with not creating a cumulatively detrimental effect on the environment such that we would leave our children and grandchildren with an inheritance of our problems? The ultimate goal is to eliminate over time all emissions, effluents, discharges from refineries, petrochemicals complexes, operations in the North Sea, and so on that have a **negative impact** on the environment. You can argue as to what 'negative' is: negative doesn't necessarily mean zero – you could find that the resource costs in getting to zero in some cases would be enormous and the provision of those resources would itself have a negative impact on the environment – but there has to be a point where an **equilibrium**, a sustainable situation, is arrived at where there is not a cumulative negative effect building up on the environment. That is the target we have set ourselves.

How do we set about turning that objective into reality? If management of the environment is going to be anything more than superficial, if it is genuinely going to be an attempt to make **progressive improvements** towards the ultimate goal, then you have to start off by establishing a **benchmark** of **where you are**, in quantitative terms. You've got to know exactly what impact your operations, tankers, pipelines, refineries, petrochemical complexes, service stations, and terminals are having on the environment. You have to have some quantitative starting point: the whole process of advancement has to be central to stategic planning, it cannot be an afterthought; in tackling any new project, one has to consider the **environmental integrity** of that process from the outset, and make adequate provision in the design, resources planning and management operation of the process.

Equally one has to deal with the very real strategic issue of how to cope with all the **existing assets** which continue to provide the commercial basis for the business. A company like Shell UK has pipelines in operation which go back sixty years, and in those days the engineering standards were very different; generally speaking, our forebears tended to over-engineer things and make greater provision. There is the constant dilemma as to where you cut off the tail of assets, and say 'I need to replace them with the knowledge of technology that I have today, my awareness of the risks'. Environmental management has to be central to one's strategy, and equally it has to be translated into hard things like budgets, projects, project plans, designs, design standards and targets for emissions and so on. The Environmental Protection Act 1990 will require nothing less, and one has to set up 'time milestones', points at which certain standards will be achieved. Only by that means do you have a plan by which to measure **progress** (and, of course, that in turn requires feedback into one's planning as to what further resources are required); certainly our intention would be always to regard the legislation not as the end of the process but as setting the **beginning**, the starting point. In our own standards, we would be aiming to move ahead of that.

Just as the provision for environmental management has to be central to one's strategic planning thinking, so in turn it naturally requires **management commitment** from the very top: leadership is delegated down through line management (this is not something you pass to somebody or the staff side of the business); concern for the environment has to be an essential part of the task of line managers from the top to the bottom of the organization. Adequate resources have to be provided, people have to be trained who are competent in this area. There has to be a genuine commitment of effort, training skills, and resources to back the concept. **Environmental auditing** is of course an extremely valuable systematic technique for establishing where your processes are in relation to legal requirements and in relation to your own internally defined standards – the scope for improving things with new technology, the potential for tighter operations. These technologies are available to establish the **gap** between where you are and where you ought to be, or where best industry practice is. Any new project has to make provision for environment and environmental integrity from the outset, and making a systematic quantitative assessment of the impact of the project on the environment is an essential aid to sound planning.

In the oil industry, we are all too well aware that it is not just the insidious day-to-day effect of operations on the environment that has the impact, but occasionally there is a major environmental emergency – the tanker spill, the pipeline spill, the refinery fire, and so on. A vitally important part of our provision for managing the environment has to be the provision of plans for dealing with just such an emergency effectively. Contingency planning – being prepared, regularly testing such plans, making sure resources are available, and so on – is just as much a part of managing the environment as longer-term planning and operating. In our business, the application of **technology and technological support** is a crucial input to the process.

How can business play its part in reacting, systematically and rationally, to the foundations established in the 1990 White Paper? I would suggest that responsible management of the environment requires business to play its part in **systematically managing the risks** of its operations, activities and projects on the environment − the risks that inevitably go with undertaking any activities. You can't avoid risks, but you can manage them responsibly, and you can reduce them to an acceptable level given current awareness. That requires the management of resources; the planning of resources and commensurate benefits; and of course it requires the harnessing and the **application** of technology.

Questions and Answers

Q   John Garbutt (Nicholson, Graham and Jones)
As long as I can remember, Shell has had a strong environmental policy; what makes this new initiative so fundamentally different?

A   To go back ten years, for the sake of argument, the big difference now is the awareness of the global impact of CO_2 (greenhouse gases or the greenhouse effect), and the concept of 'sustainable development' which has also developed over the course of the last (say) ten years. I deeply believe that, given the climate of opinion in which we operate, the awareness of these problems, and the knowledge of the environment standards set by government, we have remained at the forefront. What is new is the concept of seeing ourselves on a path of *progressive improvement* towards zero or even negative impact − i.e., our version of 'sustainable development': we are planning to arrive at a point where we can say that the oil industry is now in that situation.

Reference

This Common Inheritance (1990) Cmd 1200 (London, HMSO).

7 ICI and the Environment

Chris Hampson

Good environmental performance is good business. That is the first simple fact that lies behind ICI's commitment to upgrade its environmental performance. Environmental performance is not an optional extra, it is not even an additional cost; it is a fact of business life and those companies which tackle the issues most effectively – and, equally importantly, most efficiently – will be the winners in the business competitive race.

Why is this? What has happened to transform environmental issues from being the concern of nature lovers, idealistic students, and a few embryo 'green' groups, to having a place in the forefront of the general public's concern? I believe it is the realization that our actions can have – and are actually having – an impact not just on local surroundings, but on the Earth itself: this global concern is not a temporary phenomenon or a fad; it is here to stay. We all know that business does best when it best meets the needs of its customers, and when it responds best to market place direction. This direction is clear, and business is (in some cases, somewhat belatedly) recognizing that being environmentally responsible and responsive is one of the keys to future success. Hence my statement that good environmental performance is good business.

But industry has often done itself no favours by appearing to be unresponsive and uncaring: by stressing the difficulties of possible remedial action, or the cost; by emphasizing the confidentiality or proprietary nature of its processes or products. What industry may have seen as necessary commercial secrecy, the public interpreted either as arrogance, or as knowing we were causing pollution but not being willing to admit it – or, perhaps, even worse, not knowing what damage we were causing but being unwilling to face up to it.

This perception has masked the very real contribution industry has made to solving environmental problems. We have forced the public to conclude that:

- We don't **recognize** the problems.
- If we recognize them, we attempt to **downplay** them.
- If we are forced to do something, we will **procrastinate** as long as possible.

We in industry know that this is not a true picture, or at least not totally true. But the public's view is clear: they don't trust us, and they see industry (and particularly the chemical industry) as part of the **problem**, not part of the **solution**.

The statistics are revealing. A 1989 MORI poll showed that more than eight out of ten members of the public (84 per cent) agreed with the view that British companies did not pay enough attention to their treatment of the environment, including 43 per cent who strongly agreed. In a 1989 poll conducted for the Chemical Industries' Association, 69 per cent of respondents regarded the chemical industry as contributing to environmental problems – and this after several years of concerted effort through education, public relations and media campaigns to change that image.

This is not an issue where the industry is going to succeed with words: the public intuitively pays more attention to what we **do** than what we **say**. This implies that the industry must make sure that the positive actions it is taking are recognized: where we have a good story, we need to tell it. And where we need to improve our performance still further, we need to do it *and* be seen to be doing it. We must be **visible** and be seen to be **accountable** for our performance if we are to achieve public credibility.

While regulation is important, it is not the only (and in fact, may not even be the most) important, element in bringing about environmental improvement. **Public opinion** as expressed in market forces has a major role, so that companies act through enlightened self-interest and the carrot of business success rather than the stick of regulatory penalties. The 1990 Government White Paper clearly recognized the importance of market forces as well as regulation. Undoubtedly there are some areas where market mechanisms could be sharpened by government action, and we need to examine this in an open, constructive debate. But the market, when given a chance and the right tools to establish values, is very powerful.

I believe a successful environmental programme for any business must contain seven key elements:

- Clear leadership from the top and **management commitment**
- An explicit and widely publicized **policy** and clear **objectives**
- Measurement of **performance**
- Involvement of all **employees**
- Communication and dialogue with the **public**
- Integration of environmental considerations with **business considerations**, both technical and commercial
- **Education**.

Leadership

Of all these, the key as in so many issues in business, is the first one, the issue of **leadership**. In ICI, the Chairman has provided that leadership. Recognizing the importance of environmental issues, he established a Board position with special responsibility for environment matters, almost as soon as he became Chairman and in advance of most other companies. He made the environment one of the key issues in the statement of Group Purpose which states explicitly that ICI will achieve its aims by 'operating safely and in harmony with the global environment'. He encouraged a clear statement of Group Environmental Policy, and established clear objectives and an action plan to which the Group is now committed. The Executive Team reviews Group environmental performance at regular meetings, and the full Board also has taken a major interest. So no-one within ICI is in any doubt of the commitment to high standards, and improved performance. (The Chairman of DuPont, one of ICI's competitors, describes himself as DuPont's 'chief environmentalist'; this visible commitment is a key element in establishing credibility both internally and externally.)

Commitment is, however, one thing; **action** is the vital ingredient. And for action there must be a clear policy or framework within which the diversified parts of the Group can work, and objectives which foster clear plans. In ICI we have, apart from the statement in our Group Purpose, a clear Policy Statement which commits the Group to minimizing our environmental impact, to cooperation with government bodies, to passing on technical information to customers, licensees, and so on. It also lays out

clear lines of responsibility and accountability for **environmental performance** so that there can be no doubt where that rests.

Objectives

Our objectives are equally clear. For example all operations:

- Must comply with **existing** or **impending regulations**
- Use the highest standards of **environmental performance** in all new
  plants, even where this considerably exceeds local requirements
- Make specific reductions in the **production of waste** from our plants
- Design new plants (where possible) to **eliminate waste at source**, or
  to recycle waste streams inside plant boundaries
- Promote **recycling and recovery** of our products wherever possible –
  it is, in fact, a growing requirement of our customers that we provide
  the means of doing this
- Step up our **energy conservation** activities.

These objectives are used to set **environmental improvement goals**
within each business unit or site. We ask all operations, for example, to
report on their compliance, which effectively means 100 per cent compliance with regulations every time a measurement is taken. With nearly
20 000 measurements a year, that is not easy, but by measuring our
performance and analysing it, it is possible to pick out problem areas and
deal with them. Similarly, in waste reduction we must first identify **where
all the waste comes from**. This step alone, applied in a vigorous way,
throws up areas of further work to which resources can be applied to
achieve the objective. Setting high standards is important: unless
employees feel that the goals are real, they will not apply the innovation
and creativity we need in order to achieve them. I have no doubt that the
imperative is there, and that the risk of not acting is greater than that of
acting.

Measurement of Performance

Here, the key issue is that of establishing clear data on **what is actually
happening**: if you can't measure it, you can't manage it. The simple act of
measurement almost inevitably brings action and progress.

In the late 1980s, ICI set out to audit its environmental performance as group, and established initially four simple parameters:

- **Compliance** with regulations
- Number of serious **losses of containment**
- Complaints from **local community**
- Progress towards **environmental improvement** goals.

Getting this data, by itself, forced people to start **recording** it: the very ac of reporting motivated people to improve. No-one likes to report 'nc progress', and the data collection forced more investigation and remedia action. This is investigation and action at the local level, not centrally; there are not the resources or ability to take action in individual businesses o sites, but the reporting mechanism forced the decentralized units to take action on their own.

The next step is to make more information available to the **public**. There is a high degree of nervousness about how such information might be used (or, rather, mis-used) but I personally think we must encourage a more oper and informed dialogue, and that the steps we have taken contribute in a positive way.

Employee Involvement

Our own employees are in many ways a key audience for our environmental efforts. They actually know better than most what we are doing, and are in a position to help us improve our performance (where that is ar operational matter), or to identify the nub of many issues: they, themselves, are increasingly 'environmentalists'. One of the common fallacies stated by the media is that all 'greens' are anti-industry, and all industry people are 'anti-green': this is simply not true — often the most vocal criticisms of our performance come from our own employees. For both these reasons, we need to involve them more. In 1989, a *World in Action* programme[2] produced by Granada TV set out to show that ICI was behaving improperly in an environmental sense in the North of England. We should have suggested to our employees that they watched the programme, and given them our response to its claims; we didn't do so, and they were dismayed and upset when people who had seen the programme attacked them next evening in their local pubs for being part of such a wicked organization. At the 1990 London Conference on the Ozone Layer we communicated directly to all employees in the UK the facts, our position on chlorofluorocarbons (CFCs), and the reasons for it, and what we were doing, The company's highest priority, identified at a 1990 meeting of the Group Environmental Advisory Panel, is now to involve employees even more.

Communication and Dialogue

But employees are only one of the audiences with which we need to communicate. There are others – such as the **local communities** in which we work, the **general public**, **educational** authorities, the **environmental** organizations, and so on. We have done this historically with local communities and it is in fact a clear responsibility in our local managements to do this. The importance and scope of this dialogue is increasing; we have had a series of very successful 'Open Days' in which we have invited the public into our plants and shown them what goes on. Many (probably the majority) have never been inside a chemical plant before, and are often quite surprised in a positive sense at what they find. Our own employees have played a major role in extending our reach into the community, and can help us still further, but I believe we must do more. Some of our competitors in the USA have set up **community advisory panels**, involving a wide range of viewpoints, to advise them on environmental matters. They involve these panels in a way that gives them the full background against which judgements need to be made. This appears to have been successful in bringing a greater understanding at the plant level of what the community concerns really are, and conversely at the community level that issues are not as one-sided as they sometimes appear. Our Australian company has established a broadly-based community advisory group and I suspect ICI may want to extend this concept.

ICI would like to establish a better dialogue with **environmental groups** – I don't believe our present adversarial relationship serves either party well, and certainly is not helpful in establishing the sort of consensus necessary to move forward on solutions to our more pressing environmental problems. We in the industrial world, and many environmental groups, are aiming at the **same objectives**; I believe we all agree on the need for rapid progress on water, soil and air pollution, on the elimination of environmentally harmful products, on the benefits of not producing toxic wastes and so on. What we don't agree on usually is the **rate** at which this can be accomplished, and the **way** it should be done. Better dialogue might bridge this gap – and, more importantly, might bring about some **new thinking** and innovative **solutions**. ICI's Agrochemicals Business established with other groups a special study team to look at the problem of agrochemical regulation and residues in food. This group (which include Friends of the Earth, The Women's Institute and the Transport and General Workers' Union (TGWU)) was able jointly to arrive at recommendation which they put to the government concerning regulatory proposals. No only was this a very powerful voice to government, but the differen parties found in working together a quite surprising amount of commor ground.

I believe that we need to extend these contacts: it is already happening but not enough. Unfortunately, some environmental groups don't feel the have anything to gain by a dialogue with industry, taking the view tha confrontation is their best approach, and the more adversarial and spectacu lar, the better. We have tried to take the initiative but so far have beer rebuffed; I believe we must persist and hope that good sense and publi opinion – which increasingly seeks solutions and not just restatements o the problem – will prevail.

Integration of Environment and Business Concerns

Equally vital is the **integration** of environmental issues with all aspects o the corporation's activities, from strategy formulation, planning, construc tion through production and into dealings with our customers. There is nc doubt that environmental considerations will open new business opportu nities in the development of new technology. ICI has developed a new typ of electrolytic cell for the production of chlor-alkali which eliminates the need for using mercury or asbestos, both constituents of previous pro cesses, and both with environmental problems; the new cell is also more energy-efficient. The company has now sold or licensed this developmen to over twenty companies world-wide. Similarly, there is a process fo manufacturing ammonia which won an environmental award in 1989 anc which is now being offered for licence around the world.

On the **product** side, environmental problems require innovative solu tions such as the company's replacement for CFCs. ICI has also developec water-based paints to eliminate the use and loss of solvents, an ignitior improver for use with methanol fuels to reduce pollution, and a nev tanning chemical which eliminates the use of chrome: all these product have emerged into the market place as a result of environmental demands Almost all business will in fact be affected to a greater or lesser degree by environmental considerations and unless they are sensitive to thes influences they will lose out in the competitive race.

It is crucial for companies to realize that there are real opportunities ir environmental developments for those companies ready to recognize them. ICI intends to be one of those companies. The world requires a chemical industry, but success will go only to those participants who can meet **community** and **customer expectations**. ICI is increasingly finding ways to forge closer links with customers by adopting an attitude of product stewardship and responsible care. Customers want us to help them solve any environmental issues arising out of the use of ICI products; where we can help them we will have bonded them to us in a way that should be beneficial to both parties. It is also useful to remember that in production some environmental issues are caused by faulty or off-spec operations — incompletely reacted products, inefficient use of processing ends or raw materials, production of scrap or off-grade material, or process insufficiencies. Curing these can yield a more effective, more competitive cost structure: so it is possible to have a win-win situation.

Education

Education on environmental matters is essential, both within the company and in the public domain. Within the company we have run training courses, seminars and special technical sessions all dealing with environmental matters. Our own employees need to be made aware of the way the community thinks, as well as what we can do about it. We regularly have guest speakers at these seminars drawn from the environmental movement to make our employees see us as others see us, and then equip ourselves better to meet community expectations. But there also needs to be more education in the **public**. Views about environmental matters are imparted to students in an idiosyncratic way, reflecting the individual views of the teacher; this can lead to a one-eyed view of the matter, from whichever side it happens to come. The environment is a complex subject, and if people are to grow up making the best choices for them and their descendants, they need to have a proper understanding of the subject.

Environmental considerations bring very large costs which in the end the **community** bears. The 1990 White Paper showed that the cost of improvements to the water and sewage disposal systems alone in the UK will require £28 billion investment to the year 2000; that is investment which cannot be made elsewhere. The chemical industry is investing around £650 million per year in safety, health and environment projects, about one-quarter of total industry investment. These are large sums, and one way or another will be borne by the community; we must ensure that what we do is money well spent, and that it does produce the required effect: it would be tragic if we bore the cost but did not receive the benefit. This requires an **informed public debate**, and industry must play its part in the education process.

Regulation

There is no doubt that regulation has a role to play, but more can be achieved by motivating companies to **improve themselves** than by regulation alone. Regulation sets a lower boundary on performance; it doesn't stretch the limits of man's ingenuity. It has a place, particularly in establishing international standards: it is difficult to believe we would have made the same progress on CFC replacement without the Montreal Protocol and its 1990 London extension. But if we carry regulation too far it may stifle innovation or improvement, not enhance it. The government's approach in the White Paper recognizes the need for a sensible mix of regulation and market mechanisms, though I regret that the White Paper made no mention of the very great progress made by industry on a voluntary basis. Accomplishing the many tasks which the White Paper has identified will be a challenge, but it is only business and industry which can marshall the resources to accomplish this task and the government (and others) should be encouraging their participation in every way possible.

If there is a final message for business it is this: help **open up the communications**. Communication is a **two-way process**, it is not just a question of getting our message over to the public, it is listening and absorbing **what the public is telling us**. We must be sure and open about where we are, and where we are going: it is only with this understanding that the public will tolerate the journey from here to there. We must be able to demonstrate progress – there is no substitute for action: the public looks at what we **do**, not just what we **say**.

The Conference was about the 'Greening of Business', but business is part of the community; so we are talking about the 'Greening of the Community'. Business has a role as the means by which the community can go 'green', as the engine which focuses resources on the issues. Business is used to change – the chemical industry particularly; we have grown and prospered through change and we have a major role to play in this case. For we are faced with a great challenge – no less than changing the world in which we live. If that is what is meant by the 'Greening of Business', then industry must prepare to meet it.

Questions and Answers

Q   Iain Taylor (British Gas plc)
    What publications has ICI produced to aid in the education process?

A   There is a booklet called *ICI and the Environment* (1990).[3]

Q   David Gilliatt (paper industry)
    ICI is a high-profile company prone to examination by the media. As a matter of corporate policy do you seek to involve – or even attract – the media, so that they take an interest in ICI?

A   The company meets with the environmental correspondents of the newspapers. We try to provide the media with background information by having lunches and meetings even when there isn't any specific issue, just to explain what we are doing and how we are going about it, in the hope that when something comes up that they want to write about, they are better informed; we do that regularly. We have also taken them to visit our plants so they can see what we are doing. It's a matter of educating them as well as the public, and we put considerable effort into that. Sometimes it's helpful, sometimes it isn't, but in general I think it's the right approach. We used to have a policy of 'keep your head down' and 'least said, soonest mended', and that sort of thing, but about 1987 or 1988, we changed. Now, we don't go out to seek opportunities, but when somebody asks us to appear on a programme, we are more likely to accept than not. It's a policy that has had its pluses and minuses. ICI is very high-profile on CFCs and we talked a lot about them. There are a couple of other companies which have not said anything and there are a few people in ICI who said 'why are we up there making everybody think we are the kings of CFCs when there are other people who are just as big and who are not saying anything?' In the end, though, I believe that we need to follow this policy of greater openness and greater dialogue and that it will pay off. But we don't expect it to be all smooth going.

Q   Joe Rogaly (Conference Chairman)
    Which would you say in reality, never mind the perception, was (apart from ICI) the 'greenest' chemical company in the world?

A   That's a hard question to answer. I don't think there is actually an enormous difference between the leading chemical companies and what they actually do. Where there has been a difference has been in the way in which different companies publicize their activities, and the way they portray them to the public. My firm belief is that you've got to get out and say what you are aiming at, and be much more open about it. The public will then tolerate your performance in getting from here to there; but if you start from a position (which I think ICI started from) saying 'it's all terribly difficult, you've got to realize the problems', and so on, then you are seen as foot-dragging and recalcitrant even though you may be doing exactly the same thing. As to the companies which have had the best environmental performance overall – if you include public relations and creating the right image – I think I would have to put DuPont as close to the top as any; they've done a very good job of positioning themselves favourably in the public's mind. When we look at what they do and what we do, there is not very much difference, but they have put their activities across more effectively and that's not unimportant.

Notes

1. **Chemicals in a Green World** (London, Chemical Industries Association, 1990).
2. **'How Green is this Giant?'** (Granada TV, December 1989).
3. Available from ICI, External Relations Department, 7 Millbank, London, SW1P 3JF.

Reference

This Common Inheritance (1990) Cmd 1200 (London, HMSO).

8 Selling Corporate 'Greenness'

Reginald Watts

Despite all the hype, we must not assume there is a groundswell of change in British business. Experience shows that the speed of change on issues such as social responsibility, consumerism, and the environment are governed as much by the **economic health** of the industry concerned as by public pressure on government. Think back to the Nader days of pressure on the US motor industry in the 1960s: we forget how long ago it started.

The difference this time is that **public attitudes and values** have changed in parallel with the pressure groups; this has had a marketing impact which has concentrated the minds of business. However, despite IT and greater buying volatility among customers, there is still a tendency for manufacturers (especially in the business-to-business sector) to respond slowly to unspecified customer pressure. In the experience of BWP Consultants, our environmental communications company, most manufacturers are making the right noises but responding at **technical level** only, where legislative pressures are forcing them to do so.

Responding to Change

The fact is that public values are going through a period of massive change: the 'hippy generation' of the 1960s cut their hair, put on suits and are now mortgaged to the hilt and holding down senior jobs. The whole world of the 1960s didn't don kaftans and beads but everyone felt the influence; that influence has now moved through as the 1960s' students become 1990s' managers. Interest in the environment is thus biased towards the older members of the public, a sector which is not only growing in size demographically but also, on the 'empty nester' count, has high disposable income. Magazines are full of examples of large companies – usually multinational corporations (MNCs), as this is where social responsibility leadership tends to come from – who have invested heavily in action that is environmentally friendly; this means that change will happen, although the compression of the time frame may have slowed as a result of the economic downturn.

How should British companies and organizations respond?

- The first rule is **not to respond in isolation**. A good eco-audit will, from a communications point of view, start upstream at corporate strategy level; this is not only because the environment is a boardroom matter, but because communications is about **corporate positioning** and until that has been agreed one of its ingredients (i.e., the environmental dimension) should not be examined in isolation.
- The second rule is to be clear when you are operating with a **marketing** goal in view and when for the sake of **corporate image** – or, indeed, when the action is **pure altruism**. There's nothing wrong with environmental action for marketing or corporate image reasons, but don't pretend internally that it's altruism! The effect of muddling the objectives is to achieve none of them – or, worse, to generate a situation that backfires.
- The third rule is to accept that **communications has changed**: no longer is it effective to assume that all the dialogue is 'one-way'. Traditional image-building was about creating an image platform or message to be projected, then buying advertising space, public relations support and a dash or two of sales promotion, to put it across: the modern consumer is sophisticated; children start learning about consumerism and the environment in primary school.

    Modern communications involves developing relationships, generating a sense of involvement by companies; it uses market research as part of the **feedback process**, not as an aid to more aggressive selling messages. Fortunately, environmental issues are ones where corporations can become involved, can sponsor activity and can generate themes and subjects for debate that become the private property of the organization: they become **experts in that niche**.

Returning to the audit as a methodology, a means by which an effective environmental position can be developed for a company's external relations, there are five stages (see Figure 8.1).

Issues and Influence Linkage

Current and **future** environmental issues which impact on an organization's operations are reviewed within an industry framework, with analysis of **competitor policies** towards the environment. This part of Environmental Relations Analysis (ERA) is undertaken by face-to-face interviews conducted by senior consultants; it identifies factors which influence not only the managers of organizations, but also community and pressure groups, local, national and international government, investors and the man and woman in the street: it seeks to rank these 'influencers', and how they **interact**.

Aim: To provide **data** for policy and performance decisions.

Policy Assessment and Integration

Identifying the 'communications gap' between **internal** and **external perceptions** of the organization's environmental stance from the data collected from the first stage; this highlights **areas of practice** which give rise to concern.

Aim: To **redefine** corporate policy and objectives on all relevant environmental issues.

Technical Performance Review

To review the organization's environmental performance in the **physical environment** by an Environmental Impact Analysis (EIA), and assess its operations in areas such as safety, response to legislation, energy efficiency, etc.

Aim: To define an organization's **standards of environmental performance** and to provide a baseline for overall strategy formulation.

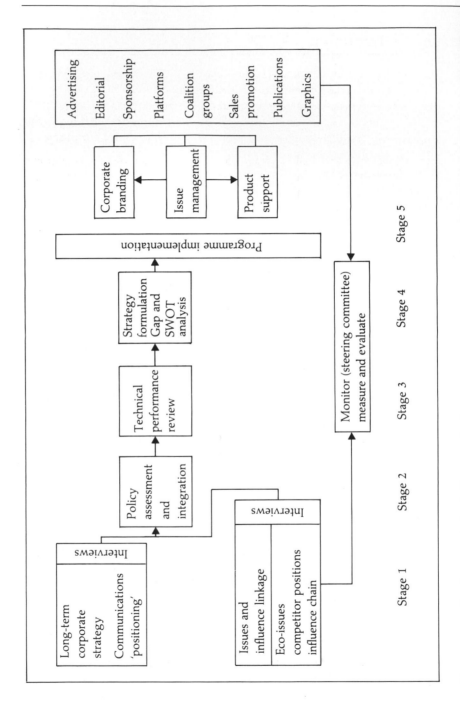

Figure 8.1   Environmental relations analysis

Strategy Formulation

To develop an environmental Gap and SWOT analysis (of **internal** Strengths and Weaknesses, and **external** Opportunities and Threats) for the organization, using both the technical review and policy assessment data. This leads to the formulation of the **environmental strategy**; the strategy will be developed to meet the policy objectives set out above.

Aim: The strategy will be used to **coordinate** all the organization's activities which impact on the environment – including marketing, communications, production and human resources.

Programme Implementation

- To correct **negative perceptions** of an organization by modifying behaviour and operations impacting on the environment.
- To establish an **environmental training programme** for the organization's staff.
- To capitalize on **environmental strengths** in external marketing and communications activities for key targets.
- To implement a **crisis management programme**.
- To maintain awareness of **competitor activity**, **legislation** and **opinion-former attitudes**

Aim: The implementation of the **strategy recommendations** combined with a **rolling evaluation and review** of the company's operations.

These five stages will lead the Board of the company towards a communications programme for some years ahead if the process is **monitored strategically**, and not left as a tactical exercise.

Selling corporate 'greenness' rests finally with the Chief Executive officer: it is now a permanent part of his or her constituency, and should be under his or her **leadership**. The **tactical action plan** must:

- Create a corporate position that generates relationships with 'movers and shakers', a better understanding of management's aims, strengths of the company – and, above all, **sells products**.
- Ensure that **product support fits corporate** strategy by establishing a steering committee.

- Set company **aspirational standards higher than legal require-ments**.
- Use advertising, press editorials, speaker platforms, published bro-chures, annual reports, sponsorship and sales promotion as a chain of communication under **one message umbrella**.
- Be **proactive** – despite the risks – not **reactive**: **Building** good public relations takes years; **destroying** it takes a day.

Corporate communications has become an integral part of every company's long-term business plans: it is no longer the message carrier **but the message itself**.

Index